OF SILENCE

BOB SCHALLER

ROAR OF SILENCE

Bob Schaller, Roar of Silence

ISBN 1-887002-85-5

Cross Training Publishing
317 West Second Street
Grand Island, NE 68801
(308) 384-5762

This book is manufactured in the United States of America.

Library of Congress Cataloging in Publication Data in Progress.

Published by Cross Training Publishing
317 West Second Street
Grand Island, NE 68801
1-800-430-8588
Publisher website: www.crosstrainingpub.com
Email Bob Schaller: Schallerrc@aol.com

Photo Credits:
© Lincoln Journal Star (cover)
© Eric Lars Bakke
© UNL Photography
© Denver Broncos
Family photos courtesy of Kenny Walker family

TABLE OF CONTENTS

Imagine walking into a crowded room where people are talking, and you can not hear a word.

Imagine a thunderstorm suddenly appearing from nowhere, and you rush to grab your children because you did not hear the weather warning sirens going off.

Imagine sitting at the dinner table and seeing your family talk excitedly about something that happened, but not being able to hear even a fraction of the conversation.

That imagination is Kenny Walker's reality. The native of Crane, Texas, who attended elementary school and junior high in Denver, Colorado, before returning to Crane for high school, never let his deafness slow him in his pursuit of what could be called lofty goals by anyone's standards. Walker left an indelible mark at the University of Nebraska as an All-American football player and an Academic All-Conference performer. He also brought the entire state of Nebraska into his world of deafness through educating people about the deaf community.

With a huge, muscular frame and a heart to match it, Walker is described by almost everyone who knows him as someone "special."

But all the special qualities in the world could not prepare him for the "crash" that occurred when he left the world of professional football. Football teams spend millions and millions of dollars on their players while they are still playing, but none of the weight-training equipment and medical treatment to keep them playing prepares them for life after football. As former Nebraska football coach Tom Osborne notes in this book, the applause ends suddenly and for good once the athlete steps off the field for the final time.

Ironically, it was Osborne who helped Walker get on with his life. During Osborne's retirement dinner in Lincoln in April of 1998, Walker looked at all the former Huskers in the Devaney Center. Some had played pro-football, some had not. All had to deal with life after football, whether they played in the NFL or if their careers ended the last time they stepped off the field at Nebraska.

So at the dinner honoring Osborne, Kenny Walker figured out that others had faced the dilemma he found himself facing. The end of Walker's pro-football career wouldn't seem to have come suddenly—but the fall of 1997 was the first time Walker had not reported for a football training camp since before he started high school. He doubted everything from his mental capacity to his manhood, not unlike other players who have been through similar situations.

I tried to find Walker in December of 1997 as I wrote the tribute book, *I Played for Coach Osborne*, which included heartfelt thoughts and memories of his former players. The Denver Broncos did not have a number for Walker, thus he was unfortunately left out of the book.

After attending a book signing in Chadron, Nebraska, I received a phone call from Martina Walker, Kenny's wife. Kenny wanted to write a book. There was quite a bit of irony in that call because Gordon Thiessen, the owner of Cross Training Publishing and the publisher of this book and I had talked about how great Walker's story was, and that it not only would make a good book, but that it needed to be a book. There is so much one can learn from Kenny Walker. Some of it has to do with what he faced with his deafness, but much of it does not. As Buffalo Bills coach Wade Phillips says in this book, everyone is handicapped in some way, Walker's handicap just happens to be deafness.

Kenny and I hooked up at his home in Council Bluffs, Iowa, over the course of several days in May of 1998. He made his family—wife Martina, stepson Tommy, son Bo and daughter Anna—dinner each night.

I met Kenny while he played with the Denver Broncos, when I covered the NFL for the *Scottsbluff Star-Herald* as that newspaper's sports editor. His smile, candor and honesty made him an anomaly among many of the players in the NFL.

Yet, he is human, painfully so at times. Before he married Martina, while still at the University of Nebraska, he had a child with another woman. That daughter is named Krishna. He speaks of the love he has for her and how much he misses her. But because of logistical and legal reasons, he does not see her as much as he would like to. Another legal battle Kenny has waged is his lawsuit against the Denver Broncos.

Still, those two issues are part of who Kenny Walker is, and while he does not want to hide anything, he can't talk about things which he is legally not permitted to comment on. But the Kenny Walker story is about a lot of different things and people. From being associated with top-notch coaches like Tom Osborne and Charlie McBride at Nebraska and Dan Reeves in the NFL, to having two outstanding interpreters, Mimi Mann at Nebraska and Guy Smith in Denver, Walker kept growing and learning.

Much can be learned from Kenny Walker. He is at once inspirational and compassionate, so cognizant of the value of the time given to him by special people that he makes time for any and almost all requests. While his deafness put him in the spotlight, what makes Kenny Walker who he is does not have all that much to do with deafness when it comes right down to it.

The thousands of letters he received at Nebraska and with the Broncos asked him many questions. While Walker responded to every letter brought to his attention, there are still questions he knows he might not have answered. Through this book, he hopes to do just that.

Bob Schaller, author, June 18, 1998

Memories.

I have so many memories of Kenny Walker because I played with him at the University of Nebraska and in the NFL with the Denver Broncos for the 1991 and 1992 seasons.

Unlike a lot of the other people in this book, my memories of Kenny are more from a professional standpoint—football-related situations. While we were not close off the field, I can say that Kenny Walker deeply affected my life from the moment we met at Nebraska to this very day.

There is an irony in my view of our relationship because a lot of attention was given to the fact that the Broncos asked me about Kenny on draft day in 1991. I did not do any magical tricks to get the Broncos to draft Kenny. I just told coach Dan Reeves, "Kenny can understand you, and you can understand Kenny once you've hung around him for a few minutes. You will understand his speech once you have spent some time with him. And, of course, Kenny Walker is a great football player." That was all I said to the Broncos about Kenny. They ended up drafting Kenny, although I know a lot of teams—maybe even all NFL teams to differing degrees—thought about how much an athlete with Kenny's ability could help their teams.

I always get a laugh when I hear coaches like University of Nebraska defensive coordinator Charlie McBride talk about how "Kenny can hear" more than he lets on to everyone. One time at Nebraska, Kenny was walking off the field. For a moment I forgot he was deaf, and I yelled out from quite a ways away, "Hold up, Kenny!" Well, what happened? Kenny stopped and turned around, looking at me. I had to catch myself from almost falling over. "This guy's deaf…how did he hear me?" I asked myself. I guess he picked up on the vibration or something. The guy is also very intuitive, so maybe that's what happened. Still, that day sticks out in my mind whenever I reflect on my time with Kenny.

On the field Kenny was a superb athlete. He was very, very strong. At Nebraska, he switched positions several times. In a way that just made Kenny more like everyone else because it is not uncommon for players to switch positions at Nebraska as coaches find out where they can best help the team and where their strengths lie. Kenny switched for a different reason—being deaf—but it was still something a lot of players went through because not all players end up playing the position that they are recruited for, or even the position they play their first year at Nebraska.

As far as Kenny being deaf, I had no problems communicating with him. His disability, to me, was not something I could refer to as a disability. For one thing, he is a tremendous lip reader. And even though his speech is different, you understand him after you're around him for a while.

Because of Kenny, I look at people who have any kind of a disability in a different light than I used to—I don't see them as "handicapped." I am more comfortable around people with special challenges than I was before I met Kenny. Being around Kenny really helped me see things in that regard a lot differently.

Still, there is no doubt Kenny has always had to work a little harder, especially considering his situation. But he did great academically and still kept up with football. For anyone to be an All-American on the field and an All-Conference student in the classroom is quite an accomplishment—it is something very hard to do. To see Kenny do it, you have to understand how hard he had to work, and you really appreciate him even more. He also compensated for his deafness in other ways. The best example I can think of is watching how a quarterback tries to call out the signals differently to draw defensive linemen offsides. Kenny started the play by watching the ball, so he was never penalized for being offside. Yet, a lot of guys who could hear would always be offside. So Kenny turned a potential weakness into a strength.

That is the philosophy he has used throughout his life, and it is one from which we can all learn.

Kenny affected my life off the field, especially as we teamed together on the Broncos. I have a cousin who is deaf, and my mother picked up some sign language. My family lives in Michigan, and there is quite an established deaf community up there. Whenever I talk to someone from back home, they always ask about Kenny, how and what he's doing, that kind of thing. He was a role model for the deaf community in a way that few people can understand.

He is also an inspiration to anyone facing a challenge. Anyone can look at Kenny's situation, see what he's done and the attitude he has kept and say, "I can do whatever I set my mind to do." Kenny is about hard work and dedication and fitting in with everyone else because he refuses to be treated as someone who is different.

CHAPTER 1

THE GRAVEL ROAD

*D*ecember 21, 1997, somewhere just outside of Shenandoah, Iowa, on a gravel road just off of a small state highway: Not even an hour earlier, Kenny Walker and his wife Martina had put their children—Tommy, Bo and Anna—in the back seat of Kenny's white 1996 GMC Sierra Extended Cab pickup truck, loaded a couple of bags in the back of the truck and headed for Martina's family home in Shenandoah, Iowa.

Now, Kenny Walker found himself holding a loaded shotgun on a lonely dirt road. His wife and children were in the truck. Kenny was, at once, a few feet away and an entire world removed from the family he doted over so often.

Kenny Walker battled deafness and the odds against him that came with it. All of a sudden the man who never quit wasn't trying any longer.

Kenny Walker, once known for his exploits as a man who overcame deafness to earn All-American honors at the University of Nebraska and then play five years of professional football, was trying to get to know himself again. During the week leading up to the trip to Martina's family home in Shenandoah, Kenny Walker wasn't sure who he was, much less where he was headed.

Kenny had a break from his job at the Iowa School for the Deaf, but wasn't enjoying his Christmas vacation very much. He knew he was not in the right frame of mind to spend time with Martina's family.

Martina recollected, "It was going to be Christmas, for all practical purposes. We were fighting because of the house. We were getting ready to leave, and Kenny was depressed."

As questions wove a web of confusion in Kenny's head, he didn't want to leave the house. The cloud of uncertainty, he thought, surely would follow him wherever he went.

"I didn't want to go," Kenny said. "It was cloudy and cold. The ice was not cold enough to go fishing, so I hadn't fished all year. The weather was awful. There was nothing to do. I hadn't found a gym to go workout at. I would look at myself in the mirror. I was no longer the muscle-guy who had played football at Nebraska and then in the NFL and the Canadian Football League. I looked at myself and thought, 'Am I a man?' I had no bulk or muscles any longer. I was being selfish. I thought, 'Is this just an ego thing?' I kept looking in the past, and not into the future."

Since Kenny no longer knew himself, the last thing he wanted to do was to go out of the house and see other people, especially ones who might recognize him.

"I hated to go out," Kenny said. "I would be embarrassed. I don't know why. I was not the football star everyone knew any longer. I slept all the time and lay around the house. It just seemed like there was nothing to do."

Not one to shun housework—even in college at Nebraska, Walker got on his roommates constantly to help him keep their house clean—Walker found himself bathing in a sea of self-pity.

"Usually, he would do housework," Martina said. "But during Christmas vacation, he stopped doing everything. The kids were bored out of their minds. I'd say, 'Take them out.' He said, 'I can't; money's too tight.' I said that he didn't have to spend money; there are the museums and the library. He just kept complaining about there being nothing to do."

Kenny interjected, "I didn't like that month."

Every time Martina suggested something to get him in the holiday spirit, Kenny shot it down before the words left her mouth. He ignored her by turning away, the deaf person's way to tune somebody out.

"He was on vacation, but I was still working 8 a.m. to 5 p.m.," Martina said. "He didn't want to wrap presents or anything. I had a few presents and wanted him to sit in front of the fireplace and help me wrap them, but he was not going to have anything to do with the holiday spirit. He'd sit in the bedroom and eat alone."

The house the family had recently moved into—which they still live in—is in Council Bluffs, Iowa. It is a relatively large house in a nice neighborhood, but to Kenny, it was a prison.

"The house wasn't perfectly clean, which is strange for me

because my whole life I always enjoyed cleaning," Kenny said. "But I didn't feel like it was home yet. We were always gone, so we didn't take care of the house. I like to stay home and be relaxed. She likes to go, go, go. I'd often say, 'There's nothing wrong with the house, why can't we stay here?'"

Kenny then decided not to beat around the bush, and in the process started stepping on Martina's toes every time he opened his mouth.

"Marti, I just want to tell you that I wish you would clean the house," Kenny told her.

Martina had heard enough.

"I can't believe this," she said. "Who makes the doctor's appointments? When you were playing football, who took care of the kids?"

The whole situation was not good and was showing no signs of improving.

"He wasn't going anywhere, and he was yelling at me about not doing more," Martina said. "When he said that, I got so mad. He got mad because I was mad."

Still, the Walkers packed for the trip. Martina thought Kenny might snap out of his funk when they reached Shenandoah.

They left on Interstate 80 and hit I-29 before heading to Highway 34. After hitting Highway 59 and heading south, the pair was in another argument as Anna sang and Bo and Tommy read.

"I am going to just go back home," Kenny said.

"Our kids know they are going to their grandparents' house," Martina signed to Kenny. "Don't ruin it."

Martina's hands were moving furiously.

"I was yelling in sign language," Martina said. "The kids didn't know what was going on because we weren't talking, just signing."

Martina tried a final time to snap Kenny out of his mood.

"You are just being so selfish," she signed to him.

Kenny was ignoring her, turning away and not watching her hands, meaning he could not "hear" what she was saying.

"I decided to just not try to talk to him anymore," Martina said. "Everything I said would lead to more arguing. He started going too fast, and I didn't react. He was trying to get my attention by speeding, but since he was ignoring me, I wasn't going to acknowledge him."

"She still doesn't understand how angry I am," Kenny thought to himself.

Only 15 minutes from Shenandoah, Kenny pulled over to the side of a gravel road near a fishing bridge next to Pirate Lake.

"Oh great, what are we up to now?" Martina thought to herself.

Her family was expecting them, and at that point, Martina just wanted to get there. Kenny put the truck in park, took the keys out of the ignition and put them in the front right pocket of his blue jeans.

He got his rifle out of the back of his truck.

Kenny picked up the first of three Winchester Dove and Quail Load shells and put it in his rifle.

He looked at Martina.

As he loaded the second bullet, Martina fumbled through her purse. She had a set of keys to the truck. While Kenny's behavior was scaring her, it was so out of character for him that she could not believe—even with the dark circumstances—he would ever harm her or the children. At the same time, she reasoned, since he is so out of character, who knows what his next move will be.

He loaded the third and final bullet into the weapon and looked at Martina. She was still watching him in the rearview mirror, and even though she turned away when he looked up after loading the gun, he knew she was watching.

"We were making eye contact," Martina said. "When he walked around the back, he looked at me.

"The way he would take the bullet out and look up at me was eerie," Martina said. "We were making eye contact, so I thought he was telling me that he was coming at me."

Martina had not seen Kenny in this kind of mood. She was more worried about the children than she was for herself, yet knowing Kenny had never shown any indication that he would hurt them.

"I knew that Kenny would not lay so much as a finger on our kids, and I had no reason to ever fear that he would hurt me," Martina said. "But you know how people snap."

At that point, Bo knew something was going on.

"What's Daddy doing?" Bo asked.

It was a question Martina would have loved to know the answer to as well. But she answered not as a potential victim, but as a mother.

"Daddy is checking his gun," Martina said. "Don't worry."

Why should Bo worry? His mother was worrying enough for everyone in the truck.

"I had the keys in my hand, and I might have been able to make a split-second decision to jump in the driver's seat and take off," Martina said. "But for as odd as Kenny was acting, I thought to myself, 'What if he's not doing anything? What if he just got out to settle down and cool off? He's in a bad mood now, and I don't think it will improve if he has to walk 20 miles to my parents' house.'

"He started walking around the truck, and I was scared," Martina said. "I was within a second of turning around and looking at him again to see what he was doing. But he came alongside the truck. The next thing I heard were the shots."

Kenny fired the shots into a tree.

"I thought about throwing the gun in the river—but my father had given it to me," Kenny said. "I don't know why I behaved that way. Firing the gun brought a sense of relief, like throwing a rock into the water or hitting a wall, something like that. Really, I didn't need the rifle anymore because at that point, I had figured out that material things were not that important."

Kenny put the gun away in the back of the truck, and the family drove on to Shenandoah. Although Anna was still singing, the ride was mostly silent.

While Kenny had felt he had gotten a needed release, Martina sat quietly, tears running down her face. In an effort not to draw attention to herself, she neither wiped the tears nor sniffled.

"They weren't tears of fear," Martina said. "I was just thinking that I had put up with more than one person should ever have to put up with. We were arguing, and he was fighting depression."

The couple had been through so many good times, but the dark cloud hanging over their relationship blocked out any thoughts of more pleasant times.

"For some reason, taking those shots at the tree really calmed Kenny down," Martina said.

"That's when I decided I had to get my life together," Kenny said. "I read about letting things go and moving on. It was a story about a soldier who had written a book to deal with his problems and let them go—to put it all behind him. My mind told me that I had to forget everything that was bothering me and move on. It was time to let it all go. I wished I had a lot of things that I didn't have. But then again, obviously, I had more than I needed. After that day I didn't have the desire to get any material things. I knew that I had what I always wanted, children and a family. My children needed a father. I wasn't able to have a father, and I miss that to this day. I don't want my children to grow up wishing they had a father and wondering why he wasn't there.

"After I fired the gun, I felt a sense of release," Kenny said. "Unfortunately, I knew right away that it scared Martina. She had never heard a gunshot. My mind was going every which way—a million thoughts were going through my head. They had no order to them at all. I thought, 'Why am I married to this woman, and why is she pestering me about things?' It wasn't like I was a drunk or did drugs or anything like that. And I thought since that was the case, our marriage should be fine. But there is a lot more to marriage than that, obviously."

The transition from professional athlete to the "common" man was not easy. Pro football had not ended on Kenny's terms. He was cut from the Broncos following a season where he had moved into the starting lineup. He played football in Canada with the goal of returning to the NFL. He dominated in the Canadian Football League and showed the NFL scouts that he deserved to return to their league.

As he stood on the dirt road in Iowa, he wondered what had gone wrong.

"My life was a mess, and I felt like a failure," Kenny said. "That was just how I felt. I had worked so hard for years and years, yet I was down at the bottom. And I questioned, 'How can I be at the bottom. How can I fail? I worked so hard.' Now money was tight, and we had three kids who needed clothes."

Unlike some pro athletes, Walker never got rich in the NFL, playing only two years in the very low six-figure range. A lot of that money was spent on simply maintaining a residence in Colorado when he was with the Broncos.

"All the money was supposed to be invested, but we drained and drained and drained it," Kenny said. "We had to live, and we had three kids. Moving from Colorado to Nebraska, from Nebraska to Canada and then, finally moving to Iowa was expensive."

Kenny's career and deafness had, over the years, prevented him from engaging in conversations with the average worker about money. Thus, Kenny understood little when it came to finances. He had always been into saving money, not spending it or taking out a loan.

"Kenny just didn't want any debt," Martina said. "He didn't know most people can't put 45 percent down on a $100,000 house. A lot of people get out of school and have a $50,000 debt, so Kenny was fortunate that he owed no money from school. But he didn't understand that."

Martina wanted to chat about the issues they faced. Kenny did not.

"Martina would want to talk issues out and work through them together, but I felt like I was the man of the family, that I had gotten us into these circumstances, and I would get us out," Kenny said.

Kenny and Martina decided to go bare bones that Christmas, buying gifts only for their kids and putting more feeling than finances into gifts for their family.

"It was Christmas time, and we didn't buy anything for each other," Martina said. "We bought something for Kenny's mom and for my mom and dad. We did spend some money on the kids—but it was pretty limited. Altogether, we spent under $600 for Christmas, which compared to the Christmas spending we did in the past was almost nothing."

Martina and Kenny returned from their weekend trip to Shenandoah on Monday. Martina and Kenny had barely spoken in 24 hours. Her first six words caught Kenny's attention.

"You need to go on a vacation," Martina told him. "I have to go back to work next week."

"We don't have enough money for a vacation," Kenny answered.

"Listen, you will only miss one day of work, and you have to put this thing behind you," Martina said.

Martina knew Kenny had to somehow find the light at the end of the tunnel. The day they returned from the early Christmas with Martina's family, Kenny still had yet to fully turn the corner and find the right perspective.

"On Monday, Kenny hadn't cooked dinner, the kids were still in their pajamas, and he hadn't done anything," Martina said. "He was lying in bed when I got home."

"Enough!" Martina thought to herself.

Martina called her sister, Katey.

"Kenny and Katey's boyfriend Tom, who is now her husband, have always been close," Martina said. "So I called Katey and told her to ask Tom to call Kenny and ask him if he'd go out with him for a while."

Martina got Kenny out of the house and called Kenny's mother.

"Kenny is not acting right," Martina told Julia on the telephone. "He's upset. Things are really not going well."

"Tell me what happened," Julia said.

"I love him and I care about him, and I'm not going to tattle on him," Martina said. "Can he just come down and talk to you?"

"Of course he can," Julia said.

Strapped for cash, the Walkers made some calls and found a good deal on a plane ticket, but the flight left from Kansas City, which meant Kenny had to drive three hours.

"I was able to clear my head while he was gone," Martina said. "Because of Kenny's mood, the house was so depressing. I missed him, but his absence was a relief. His moods set the whole family's mood. It was a relief."

Martina's call was enough to let Julia know that Kenny was having some difficulty.

"I was very worried about him," Julia said. "Marti had called and said he was burned out on everything. I asked her what was wrong, and Marti said Kenny told her, 'I just want to be with my mom for a while.' He came down here, and we spent a lot of quality time together. It was just like it was back when Kenny was in high school. We had breakfast, did yard work. We talked very seriously about understanding life, what marriage is about and raising children."

Kenny's mother believes a sense of healing comes from going back to where one is from.

"Maybe it was just time for Kenny to take a step back away from his life in Iowa, and touch base with where he has been and where he is going," Julia said. "He was confused and upset. After we talked, I had the feeling that just being here made a difference."

Kenny was asking questions about the long-term future. His mother told him that while the long-term is important, he has to live in the moment—both to enjoy it and deal with the consequences that one faces in the present.

"We talked about things he was planning to do in life, and he asked me what I thought about them," Julia said. "I told him, 'Kenny, if these are things that please you and make you and your family happy, you should do them.'"

While the two covered a lot of ground, Julia said the time was more relaxing than anything else. In fact, she hardly varied her routine. Kenny just fit in.

"While he was down here, he just went with the flow," Julia said.

Julia and Kenny talked about how growing up essentially without a father influenced Kenny. That spurred Kenny to think about what Tommy, Bo and Anna would go through without him in their lives.

Julia said, "Because Kenny was without a father for the most part, he feels like it is important to be around his children as much as he can. He wants to raise his children because he missed having a father figure. I just love that about Kenny. He really is such a good dad."

While Kenny was visiting his mother, he also went by his father's home.

"The first day I was in Texas, I stopped at my mother's home and my father's house," Kenny said. "My father showed me the house. The condition looked good inside. But when you looked outside, the yard was a mess."

Seeing his father—and remembering the times he didn't see his father—helped Kenny get a clearer picture of what he wanted in his own future.

"The next day, I woke in the morning and cleaned the whole day," Kenny said. "I looked at my father and wondered what it would have been like through the years to have been with him. Oh, it would have meant so much to me to have a father there. Then, I thought about Tommy, Bo and Anna, and I didn't want them to be standing in my yard in 20 years thinking, 'I wonder why Dad wasn't with us. It would have been so great to have him see us grow up.' I love my children. I don't want to miss seeing them grow up. I need them, and they need me. We love each other. I will always be there for them."

Kenny decided his father's yard needed to be cleaned.

"My father didn't like doing the yard work," Kenny said. "I looked around the yard and said, 'You need to get this yard in shape, get all this stuff out of here.' "

His father looked at him.

"Who do I need to clean it up for?" his father asked. "I don't mind it like this."

Kenny started thinking about what his father said. Even though he simply enjoyed yard work, he took more satisfaction keeping his yard in Iowa clean so his kids could play in it.

"That was a reality check for me," Kenny said. "Who did my father have to do something like that for? No one. I want to have someone—my kids—there to enjoy the little things in life with me."

So Kenny decided he'd help his father out.

"I will come and clean it up," Kenny said, "because I want to. And you will enjoy it when it is clean because it will look nice."

The hard work helped Kenny sort his thoughts out even more.

"I knocked down the fence that my grandfather built because it hadn't been kept up, and it was no good any longer," Kenny said.

While he was in Texas, Walker realized that his life lay a thousand miles away—where his heart was, in Iowa.

"I had lived away from Texas for so long, and so much had happened," Kenny said. "I realized for the first time that home was in Iowa. I love my hometown in Texas, but I knew I didn't live there any longer. My heart is with my children, and our home will be in Iowa, or any other state, but it will be together."

Back home in Council Bluffs, a couple of days passed since Kenny had flown to Texas. As Martina sat down to dinner with the kids Thursday night, the phone rang.

"I miss you," Kenny told Martina. "And I miss the children, too."

After staying through New Year's, Kenny flew back to Kansas City and drove to Council Bluffs.

"Things weren't perfect when he came back, but he knew where he wanted to be and what he wanted in life," Martina said. "There were still some arguments. There were things about me bothering him. We just weren't happy like that—it didn't turn around overnight."

Kenny's father-in-law, Dan Offenburger, said the trip to Texas was just what Kenny needed.

"Any time a spouse needs to leave the home, there is some concern, especially in your own family," Offenburger said. "But he needed to see his family. The Walker family consists of very nice people. Kenny's mother basically raised six kids on her own, and she is a tower of strength. Sometimes you just need to go back and be close to that. We wanted him to be OK; we wanted their marriage to be OK, the kids to be OK."

Martina had the same concerns Kenny did about their children needing to grow up with a father present.

"While he was gone, I was scared," Martina said. "I didn't want to be a single mom with three kids and the children having their family torn up."

The lessons were hard, as was the entire month of December in 1997. But Kenny believes the trials and tribulations were well worth the resulting maturity and perspective he gained.

"There are just some things you need to learn in life, and sometimes you have to learn the hard way," Kenny said. "I figured out that when you get married, you are together for the better and the worse—not just the better, not just the worse. I remember the feeling of my parents separating. It was not a good feeling. I had faith that Martina and I could work it out. I knew we wouldn't get divorced. We had loved each other so much for so long that there was a strong enough love there that we could work through this— or anything. I didn't want a different or new life. I have a good life here. I didn't believe in separating or divorce. Why do you divorce? Divorce is like losing, and it's also the easy way out. I don't accept losing, and I have never taken the easy way out."

Before he flew home, he had found what he was looking for.

"At that point, I dealt with the money issue that had been bothering me," Kenny said. "Money means nothing to me. Love is what matters. Money can't buy the thing that matters the most— love." Which brought Kenny back to what matters most to him— family.

Applying a simple analogy helped Walker deal with the problems he was facing, realizing the solution couldn't be pulled out of a magician's hat.

"The way I came to deal with my problems was like this," Kenny said. "In everyone's life, you have a bag of marbles. The more marbles you are able to keep in the bag, the more stable you are emotionally. The fuller the bag, the better you are mentally. What happened was I dropped the bag of marbles on the floor. They were on the floor when I left for Texas. To fix your problems, you can't just sweep up the marbles and put them in the bag and pretend that everything is fine. You have to take a step forward, and then you get one marble. You pick them up one marble at a time."

The "marbles" search is a constant process.

"So during the drive to Kansas City, I picked up one marble and put it back in the bag," Kenny said. "In Texas, through the time with my family, I was able to find another couple of marbles and get them back in the bag."

Kenny's quest for "marbles" led him back to his family in Council Bluffs, Iowa.

"Now, there aren't as many marbles on the floor," Kenny said. "Say I dropped 100 marbles in December. I have, at this point, picked up 25. I have made some steps, but I have many more big strides left to get those remaining 75 marbles."

Walker keeps moving in a positive direction.

"The hardest marble to pick up was the first one," Kenny said. "Some marbles are easier to pick up than others as I move forward. But as long as I keep heading in the right direction with my family, my spirituality and my work, things will continue to work out."

All the problems have not been completely worked out. So Walker takes life one day at a time.

"We are trying to work out the finances, which is something almost every family goes through," Kenny said. "It has been hard, but we are both working and raising our children, and we are happier now."

With Texas but a memory in life's rearview mirror, Walker is content to be thankful for what he has.

"I decided that I would build my life in the Midwest and grow as a person here," Kenny said. "We live in a nice neighborhood with very nice people living around us."

Those neighbors also like Kenny.

"The neighbors love Kenny," Martina said. "One of our neighbors had a hernia. The man is in his 50s, so his children are grown and don't live at home. He had an operation, and then it snowed. He was going out to try to shovel his drive. Kenny found out about the operation and went out and shoveled his drive every time it snowed. The guy's wife said, 'Kenny you don't need to do this. We would never ask that of you or anyone.' Kenny replied, 'I'd really like to do it. Please let me.' "

Living in a subdivision populated with kids and other family-oriented people is a natural fit for Kenny.

"When we lived in Colorado and had a snow blower, Kenny would do all of the neighbors' driveways," Martina said. "He just loves to do things that make other people feel good and put a smile on their faces, especially if one of them has gone through some adversity. That's just how Kenny is. He and his brother Gus are the same way—they mowed everyone's lawn in Crane who didn't have a lawn mower or who couldn't afford to get their lawns mowed."

Julia Walker knew her son faced challenges as a deaf person. She knew he would not lead the so-called "normal" life of others—but what does "normal" really mean? She knew that he had what it took to make it in life.

"I did not worry about Kenny never being able to leave home or not ever getting married," Julia said. "But I will admit that how his life has worked out—playing at Nebraska and being an All-American and then playing for the Denver Broncos—I never did dream anything like that would ever happen."

Kenny Walker's life is about dreams. It is also about reality. To understand where Walker was coming from on that dirt road, one has to understand where he has been, and where he is going.

CHAPTER 2

COMATOSE AT AGE TWO

Kenny Walker's mother had been excited that her youngest son would turn three years old in only six months. But as little Kenny turned a grayish color and then grew more pale as his condition worsened, Julia Walker wasn't as concerned with his third birthday—she was just hoping she'd have a healthy son come tomorrow.

"It was on a Friday night," Julia Walker said. "I was babysitting Kenny and some other children. I thought he had a cold, but Kenny got sicker and sicker. By Saturday morning, there was no question that Kenny's illness was much more serious than a cold."

Kenny, full of life and energy only a week earlier, was getting more and more listless as the days passed.

Kenny's condition worsened each day. His mother called her father-in-law, who drove them to the hospital, which was an hour away. Kenny went into a coma on his grandfather's lap.

When he was comatose, doctors tapped his spine and yellow fluid came out, indicating spinal meningitis. To get the fever down, Kenny was packed in ice on and off for a week.

"It was touch and go for quite a while," Julia said. "He went into the hospital on Friday, February 2. He came out on Friday the 13th, which is odd because you don't always think of good things happening on Friday the 13th."

When he came out of the coma, his life essentially began again.

"I was very young when all that happened," Kenny said. "But I remember seeing a lot of white light. I believe that happened when I was close to dying. It felt like I was in a tunnel traveling at a high speed."

Although Kenny survived the scare, the little boy before the coma had died in many ways. The new Kenny Walker resembled the other one only cosmetically.

"It was like a nightmare," Kenny said. "The closest thing I can say to explain what it was like—coming out of the coma—was that it was like being born twice. I had to learn to walk again. Any motor or neurological skills that I had developed in the first 30 months of my life were gone. I was back to square one. I had no memory of my life before the coma. My family told me that before the coma, I had begun to speak very well. But I don't remember that at all."

Kenny Walker, once the life of the party as he talked on and on as a two-and-a-half-year-old, was now different and would be for the rest of his life. The meningitis left him deaf—not hard of hearing, but completely deaf. On top of that, he could not speak with any appreciable clarity. Those around him could pick up on words here and there, but since Kenny could not hear himself, learning to speak clearly became that much more difficult.

"When I was young, I felt sorry for myself about being deaf," Kenny said. "There were so many things I would do that I couldn't communicate to other people. I wanted to know what people were saying when they were talking. I felt lonely."

Julia knew she had a deaf son. But she would not permit him to be mute.

"When I grew up, my mom forced me to talk," Kenny said. "I would still speak to everyone, so people could hear me. I was always forced to talk. It was hard to come home because no one signed. It seemed like no one would answer me."

Crane, Texas, lay in a rural area of the state. The resources to help a deaf child simply were not available. Julia worried about Kenny's educational prospects with no specialized teachers in the area.

"I worried about him not being able to communicate," Julia said. "I did not have a means or way to get him the attention he needed in school. Our pastor's wife helped me get to Denver and enroll Kenny in the school there."

Julia knew her son needed special attention at school. But she made a conscious effort to make sure he received no special treatment at home. She wanted her youngest boy to be just like the other kids. So she made sure his environment was no different than any of the other boys.

"He was never treated any differently by me or by the other children," Julia said. "Of course, he did need some special care because he could not hear. But as far as his upbringing, he was raised like the other children."

The family developed ways to communicate. Each person in the family created his/her own kind of language when speaking with Kenny.

"We took sign language to varying degrees," Julia said. "Kenny had a group of friends he played with. Of course, there were frustrating times where he didn't understand a lot of things. But it was never like he was an outsider."

School in Crane was very difficult for Kenny, who could not express his needs to his teacher while at the same time often missing the message the teacher was delivering to the class.

"The hardest thing was when the teacher would write on the blackboard and talk while she was doing it," Kenny said. "I couldn't understand unless she was facing me, so there was a lot of time in the classroom that was, for me, wasted time. I always had to ask teachers to repeat things. I don't blame the teachers because I don't know if they knew what they were supposed to do to communicate with me. It was a small town in Texas, and in the smaller towns— back then, especially—they didn't really know how to work with disabled kids. So I always asked a lot of questions."

The work ethic that carried Kenny Walker to the top of the college football world and then into the NFL was born out of those struggles as an elementary student. He did not want to be different. But fitting in was a daily struggle, one that forced him to be different simply by the volume of work he had to put in to fit in.

"I had to work very hard," Kenny said. "I asked my brother Gus to teach me words. He told me to look them up in the dictionary, so I spent a lot of time doing that. When you are young, you really need to know how to talk to have any chance at communicating. And when you are young, you need to communicate constantly. I could guess only about 25 percent of what people said, which sometimes wasn't even enough to get the idea of what they were saying. I had to be a follower, even though my personality was probably more toward being a leader. Communication, especially when I was younger, was really a hard part of my life."

Kenny found sustenance in the baby steps he took toward communicating with others. Still, the battle was fought daily, and the constant need to build bridge after bridge to communicate took a toll on him.

"I really felt like I was at the bottom of the ocean a lot of times," Kenny said. "To this day, I still don't really understand how I made it through the years."

How he made it through the years can be summed up in two words: hard work.

"You have to pursue some way to communicate," Kenny said. "You can't give up. That's the hardest part, knowing that you will have to take a step forward and two steps back. The light at the end of the tunnel is sometimes just a flicker, but you push and push until it gets brighter. But it does put a lot of pressure on you."

Kenny's mother Julia remembers a particular time when her son expressed the loneliness that the dearth of communication in his silent world caused.

"His third-grade class was doing gifts for mothers on Mother's Day," Julia said. "I remember the teacher had asked the parents to send paper plates to school. Kenny drew his mom, dad and his brothers on one side of the plate. Everybody had a mouth, except Kenny. The funny thing is, we never really talked about that. Kenny knew he had a mouth, but since he was unable to speak, he did not use it as much as others did."

When the family—minus Kenny's father—moved to Denver, he found his world turned upside down. He had developed ways to communicate with his friends in Crane over the years. So while Denver brought a chance for educational enrichment in a school specializing for deaf children, it brought another social challenge, at least at first.

"It was easy for me to fit in, which might sound surprising," Kenny said. "The difficult thing is developing new friends and a new life, which I had to do when we moved to Denver. The whole picture changed, and I had to develop a way to communicate with people I was meeting. That was hard because I had really learned to communicate well with the people at my school in Crane."

Kenny gained more and more appreciation for the kind of mother he had as he saw how other parents treated their children.

"On the day after school, I saw a parent show one of their kids how to give the finger," Kenny said. "That really struck me as wrong. I thought to myself, 'What are you thinking, teaching your child that? How will they respect other people when they are learning that kind of thing growing up?' "

Persistence joined Kenny's arsenal of weapons to fight deafness. And any let-up meant two big steps backward. So he kept his focus and concentration at the highest level possible on a daily basis.

"I got average grades, even though I was trying really hard and getting better all the time at lip reading," Kenny said. "The teachers treated me well. The first time I missed a class, making up work was hard for me because of the communication problem. So I made sure not to miss any more classes."

Life in Denver for elementary and junior high was rough logistically because Kenny lived in a high-crime, downtrodden area of Denver. But it was all Julia could afford, so the chance for Kenny to get the schooling he needed outweighed living in a tough neighborhood. However, it also showed Kenny a side of life he would never have been exposed to in the sleepy confines of Crane.

"It was rough at first in Denver because the kids were so tough," Kenny said. "In Texas we lived in a small town, and it was safe, not like the big city. The attitudes in small towns are just completely different from what I found in the big cities."

The academic learning was complemented by the social skills Kenny learned. While his deafness might have made him a target for bullies, his big physical build and warm smile helped him fit in for the most part. Still he nurtured the need for survival long before most kids his age had ever given such matters a second thought.

"The other kids respected me, which I think really helped me," Kenny said. "When I was young, I was too small and too smart to fight. Then I actually started being a bully. But my mother taught me self-discipline. That's important because to play football in college or in the NFL, you have to expect frustration and deal with it. And you have to be aware that you must protect yourself because there are people out there who will hurt you."

CHAPTER 3

SPORTS LEVEL THE PLAYING FIELD

Kenny's introduction to sports was as difficult as his introduction to the classroom. Since other kids didn't know Kenny very well because of his deafness, they assumed he would struggle in sports.

"When I was young, they didn't allow me to participate in sports because I was deaf," Kenny said. "When I was finally allowed to play, I was picked last. By the second day, I was picked first every time."

His mom says sports was a communication device that helped Kenny fit in with other kids because of the common interest sports provided.

"To an extent he would get frustrated, especially when he was unable to communicate," Julia said. "So in that aspect, the sports helped him make more friends, or at least spend time with the other boys and show them that except for being deaf and not speaking normally, he was no different than they were. Kenny played in the basketball league at the Boys' Club. So he went through everything the other kids did."

Basketball was an easy sport for Kenny to master. His hearing wasn't the obstacle one might have thought it to be because of the wide open nature of the game and the fact that there are only five players on a side at any one time.

"Because basketball is such a visual game, communication wasn't that difficult for me," Kenny said. "And I could tell by body language when the whistle blew—it was not hard at all for me in that regard."

Kenny's mother said the deafness was far less a factor in the world of sports than it was in the real world.

"I don't think being deaf was as big a deal as people in sports might think it was," Julia said.

The Walkers moved to Denver when Kenny started elementary school and spent the summers in Texas. They moved back to Crane when Kenny started high school.

"We went home to Crane every summer to see all of our relatives," Kenny said. "So I was fortunate to have friends in both Crane and Denver. I liked the big city because there was better competition when it came to sports. But there was the risk of living in the big city."

Ironically, the one time that Kenny was picked on came during a sporting event. It was a day he won't soon forget because he has so much regret over how he responded to it.

"I remember when kids were mean to me, especially in junior high and elementary," Kenny said. "If a kid was mean to me, I would try to not respond to it. In junior high I was suspended for three days for fighting. We were playing basketball, and we beat this team so badly that one of the boys came up to me and called me 'lame' and said that I was 'sorry.' He started to try to kick me, but he missed. I asked, 'Why did you try to do that to me?' So I hit him right in front of the principal and got the suspension. I was never a bad kid, and that didn't happen again. But by then, I was a leader in the group of kids I hung around. So I had to stand up for myself."

The 72-hour ban from school was a blessing in disguise because it gave Kenny time to reflect on how he had responded to the situation. Had he not been disciplined, he believes he might have responded the same way under similar circumstances.

"I will always remember that because I stayed home for three days, and I hated to stay home on school days," Kenny said. "I remember kids calling me names and things like that. But the kids who did that were mostly troublemakers. I didn't understand why they would pick on me, so I did all I could to not let it bother me. But if they thought of messing with my friends, I would stand up for them. I was a leader. If anyone bothered my friends, I would mess with them."

While Kenny made his name on the football field, he showed more potential—at least initially—when he played basketball.

"We used to play sports in the street, but in junior high I played basketball," Kenny said. "I never did like sympathy or look for it. From the time I was young, I was competitive. That was the case in sports and in the classroom."

Fred Walker, Kenny's father, had introduced Kenny's older

brothers to the sport. So it was only logical that Kenny pick up a basketball.

"My father played basketball, so that sport had a tradition in our family," Kenny said. "I think it was just a big part of my father's world."

When he was in junior high in Denver, Kenny started his basketball career.

"I started playing basketball in seventh grade," Kenny said. "We had a bad team. We used to lose a lot. But in eighth grade we won all the games but one, and then won five games and won first place in the all-city junior high tournament. I liked the feeling of winning."

Kenny took the lessons he learned playing basketball and applied them to his life.

"I remember when I started to learn about poise, and that helped me not only in basketball but in school and with my friends," Kenny said. "The key to developing as a team is for everyone to have poise."

Julia Walker worried about all of her sons—not just Kenny—playing football. That fear was justified when one of Kenny's older brothers went out for the sport.

"I wanted to play football my sophomore year in high school at Crane," Kenny said. "But my older brother broke his ankle playing football. My mother would not let me play football because of what happened to my brother. So I played without my mother's permission. My mother is a good person. She just wanted what was best for us. The first day of football I put the pads on. It was such a new experience because I had never done that before. I was just curious."

Football opened up a whole new world to Kenny. Although he did well in basketball, he found football to be his sport because he had to only concern himself with executing his own responsibilities on each play whereas in basketball he had to rely on others.

"Football was different from basketball because you have to compete every play against another player one-on-one," Kenny said. "I could do that, and I felt good about it. The first practice my sophomore year, I went up against a guy who was a senior and three-year starter. I ran him over like a truck. I remember thinking, 'What just happened? And how did that happen? I thought he would be stronger and better than me. What's wrong with him? Maybe I just got lucky.' So we lined up, and I did it again. Then I thought, 'I'm a good basketball player, but I've never been a football player. This guy is a senior!' So I could tell right away that I might be pretty good at football, and that helped me enjoy it, which in turn made me want to work as hard as I could to improve and get stronger."

Many coaches feared Kenny would have no clue when the referees whistled the play over, thinking Kenny might plow into some unsuspecting player. That simply was not the case.

"Being deaf didn't really ever affect me when I played high school football," Kenny said. "What happened was the coach was worried that I wouldn't hear the whistle and I'd get us penalized 15 yards for late hits. But I could always tell when the play was over by the way people carried themselves. I am still proud of the fact that I was never called for a late hit in a game. It happened once or twice in practice, but never in a game because I focused and concentrated better in games."

Being deaf did force Kenny to make certain adjustments. One of the things he did to compensate was take cues from other players— when he saw a teammate move, he knew the play had probably begun. But that wasn't always the case, so Kenny ended up paying attention to the ball instead.

"When I first started playing football, if any of my teammates went offside, I would too because I'd go on their movement," Kenny said. "Whether you have hearing or not, you are going to jump offside once in a while. You are trying to guess the snap, whether you can hear or not. But I learned to watch the ball and go off the snap, so it became easier. While noise and other sounds on the field or in the stadium affected other players, it never did get to me— because, of course, I couldn't hear it."

Julia moved the family back to Crane when Kenny entered high school. It didn't take Crane High School football coach Rickey White very long to see that, even in the small town of Crane (population: 3,533), Kenny Walker was a big-time player.

"He came to us when he was a sophomore in high school," White said. "He was just oozing with athletic ability. He had never played football before."

While White knew Walker was a diamond in the rough, Walker's glow still showed through early.

"I had a good idea he could play college ball the first time I saw him on the field," White said. "He had great ability. As a sophomore he played on the varsity. As a senior, he dominated."

There was little difficulty in communication between Walker and White. In fact, White believes he and Walker had among the best and most open lines of communication White had with any player.

"If you talk to Kenny over a period of time, you get to where you can understand him," White said. "And he is a tremendous lip reader. He catches on to emotion. He knew if I was mad or if I was happy. He really was easy to coach."

Walker's future was clearly on the defensive side of the ball because of his size and strength. But at Crane, Walker was quite an offensive weapon.

"He was awfully good," White said. "We played him on offense as a wideout, so he could see the ball. He had great size, at 6-foot-4, 225 pounds. So we'd just throw it up, and he'd go get it."

The basketball talent continued to be nurtured at Crane High School.

"What an athlete he was," White said. "He played in the Texas football all-star game and was all-state in both football and basketball."

However, after Kenny's sophomore year his brother Gus had left Crane.

"Gus had gone to Denver, and I missed him so much every day," Kenny said.

Kenny called Gus.

"I want to move back to Denver to be close to you," Kenny said. "It's not the same without you here. I miss you too much."

"No, Kenny—you have to stay in Crane," Gus told him, "or you will lose everything you have built up as a football player and basketball player."

White said while Gus and Kenny's relationship was important to both, Kenny had to make his own mark.

"He's a great young man and has been that way all of the time that I've known him," White said. "When he was a sophomore and his brother Gus was a senior, Gus took care of him as far as making sure Kenny knew his way around and got to the right class. But after Gus was gone, Kenny's personality really blossomed."

CHAPTER 4

HEADED TO TEXAS TECH

Sports was just a way to help Kenny fit in with other kids and make new friends. Now, it became apparent that sports was going to help Walker further his education.

"I realized that when I was a senior, I would probably get the opportunity to play football in college," Kenny said. "With basketball, the communication situation probably made it impossible to play in college, even though I really enjoyed playing basketball."

While the recruiters weren't knocking down doors at first, Walker was intrigued by the coaches' interest in him.

"I got a letter from a small college my junior year," Kenny said. "They were looking at me for both basketball and football."

The person Walker was the closest to growing up, big brother Gus, had moved on from Crane after graduating. Aside from his mother, there was no one around the house to talk about colleges with as the letters continued to arrive.

Since an in-state college, Texas Tech, gave Walker a chance to attend college and play football yet remain relatively close to home, Walker's decision started to look easy.

"Texas Tech invited me to come watch a football game," Kenny said. "I looked at the stadium and walked around the campus. I wasn't scared really. I just had no idea what it was like, and I wanted to learn what it was about. My life was limited at that point— because no one else in my family had graduated from college."

The visit to Texas Tech answered one important question: he would go to college.

"That visit to Texas Tech was when I realized I wanted to go to college," Kenny said.

While the other letters he received were flattering, he didn't see any other school presenting a better option than Texas Tech. So, in a way, he planned to become a Red Raider by default.

"Since I really didn't seriously consider any other offers, I was kind of excited to go to Texas Tech," Kenny said. "It was only three hours from our home in Crane, so I was a big Texas Tech fan growing up. Three people in high school my senior year were planning to go to Texas Tech, so I would know at least a few people there."

Independent because that's how he was raised, Kenny consulted with his high school coach about his college choices, but the decision on where to go was his own.

"Nobody told me what to do," Kenny said.

But one day that all changed. Kenny worked part-time during the school year as a janitor. He was sweeping in the gym to help out with the family finances when he saw a poster that would change his life.

"I saw a poster of the Nebraska placekicker that someone had put up on a wall," Kenny said. "I stood there and looked at the 'N' on the helmet. I didn't recognize it, yet it looked familiar. It brought back the memory of watching TV in Colorado when I'd see Nebraska play. Moving back to Texas, I no longer saw Nebraska games because they never showed Nebraska games in southwest Texas. In fact, the TV announcers rarely talked about the northern schools. I felt something special looking at that red 'N.' I was like, 'Yes, that's Nebraska. They were my favorite team to watch. They were always good.' I took the poster down, rolled it up, and took it home."

"From the moment I saw that poster, everything became clear," Walker said. "Getting recruited to play college football seemed like rolling the dice—I wasn't really sure what to expect at any of the other schools. But then when Nebraska came into the picture, it was like rolling a dice, and it was coming up with an 'N.' "

With the poster under his arm, Walker went to find his coach.

"I went into Coach White's office at the school," Kenny said.

"OK Kenny, there's going to come a time when you have to pick a school, just like we've talked about," White said. "So what are you thinking? Texas A&M, Texas Tech or Oklahoma?"

"Coach," Kenny said. "I am going to Nebraska."

"Nebraska, where did that come from?" White answered. "What, are you crazy or something?"

"No, Coach," Kenny said. "I just want to go to Nebraska."

"Coach White was surprised because no one wanted to go to Nebraska from down there," Kenny said. "When I was young living in Denver, my mother knew I would go down in the basement and watch Nebraska football games. It really thrilled me—just the thought of playing for Nebraska—and I don't know why. No one else in my family was a Nebraska fan."

"The way he ended up at Nebraska was odd," White said. "His mom told me to handle all the recruiting. I asked him where he wanted to go to school. He said he wanted to go to Nebraska. I picked up the phone and called Steve Pedersen, who was the recruiting coordinator at Nebraska."

"I have a kid here who wants to come to Nebraska," White said.

"Where is he going to visit?" Pedersen asked.

"Texas, Texas A&M, Texas Tech," White said, "and Oklahoma."

Looking back, White knows when he got Pedersen's attention.

"When I said Oklahoma, I heard his interest level perk up a few notches," White said.

After hearing that Walker was eyeing the Sooners, Pedersen said, "We'll send someone down to look at him."

Pedersen didn't say when. He didn't have to.

"The phone rang maybe an hour later," White said. "Nebraska assistant coach Milt Tenopir was in Midland, not far from here, recruiting Jake Young. Coach Tenopir called me on the phone, and I told him Kenny was good enough to play at Nebraska."

"I'll be there in an hour to look at some film," Tenopir said.

"He drove over that afternoon," White said. "We went into the film room, and I turned on the projector."

On the first play, Walker had a sack, racing into the backfield, shedding off a double team and throwing the quarterback down like a rag doll. On the second, he fought off two players to make a solo tackle, forcing a punt. On the punt, Walker made two huge blocks.

"Stop the projector," Tenopir said. "Can I use your phone?"

Tenopir called Pedersen.

"There's a kid named Kenny Walker here at Crane, and he can play," Tenopir said into the phone. "Go ahead and set him up for a visit."

Looking back, Tenopir said Walker was dominating.

"Kenny Walker," Tenopir said, "was all over the place on that film. It was very impressive. Every time I saw him from then on out, he just seemed to get better and better."

Tenopir was also surprised at how easily he could communicate with Walker.

"I could tell right away that he was a great athlete," Tenopir said. "Once I saw him on the film, there wasn't any question that he was a guy we'd recruit. We had concerns with having a deaf person. But he was a little different than a lot of people might expect in that it was not that difficult to carry on a conversation with him."

Besides, Walker had the qualities that Nebraska coaches always looked for: good character, strong academic standing and loads of football talent.

"He was just a likeable kid, and we built a relationship based on trust right away," Tenopir said. "He saw right away that we weren't high pressure recruiters, and he liked that. Just as important as that, he had a deep liking for Nebraska."

While Tenopir gave Walker rave reviews to Nebraska head coach Tom Osborne about Walker's football ability, Tenopir believes Walker could have played college basketball.

"I went and watched him play basketball, and that was just unbelievable," Tenopir said. "Teams would full-court press Crane, and Kenny would handle the ball and bring it up the court. He would rebound, score and pass—he could easily dunk the ball. He could do whatever his team needed him to do on the basketball court."

White started believing Walker, feeling like Nebraska was the only place for his star player.

"From the first moment I met Coach Osborne and the rest of his staff, they had a tremendous amount of class," White said. "Whenever they were recruiting, they wore ties. Yet, while they were professional, they showed a huge amount of care and sensitivity. The Nebraska coaches were just a first-class outfit all the way through."

"To me football wasn't the first thing I thought about when I picked a college," Kenny said. "Rickey White told the Nebraska coaches up front that it wasn't about football for me. Rickey always said, 'Your education is No. 1, and football is No. 2. I agreed with that. I wanted to see what each school offered. Most of the colleges focused on football first, not academics, which is something that stuck out in my mind. So when I saw the Nebraska poster and thought about the Huskers, it was kind of a last-ditch effort because the other programs hadn't shown me what I was looking for. Then I went and visited Nebraska, and it was obvious that academics were first by far."

Osborne told Walker he understood his unique situation, but that it would not hamper Kenny's chance to either get an education or play football.

"We had some concern about his situation at first," Osborne said. "But we felt whatever difficulties he had could be overcome."

Osborne made the necessary arrangements for Walker's recruiting visit.

"Coach Osborne said there would be no problem for me to have an interpreter up there," Kenny said. "I was just so happy, so moved. It was like everything I was looking for. It ended up being good that I visited Nebraska last because like the old saying goes, I was saving the best for last, as it turned out—by visiting Nebraska."

According to White, it wasn't just what Osborne said, it was how the longtime Husker coach said it that made the biggest impression.

"Coach Osborne was very sincere," White said. "Coach Tenopir did a great job of recruiting him and staying in touch with him. He couldn't talk on the phone with Coach, of course. But the coaches would call me—and I want you to understand that he was highly recruited. I'd get calls from all over the country."

White, worried about Walker, decided that he'd go along on the trip to Lincoln.

"Kenny had never flown before, so I paid my way and went with him to the University of Nebraska," White said. "There was heavy fog in Dallas, so we couldn't land at the Dallas-Fort Worth airport to make our connection to Lincoln. We had to go back and wait four hours for another flight when the fog had cleared. That's one case where I would have worried about Kenny had he been alone. Because even though the pilot announced what was going on,

Kenny couldn't hear that. He might have been wandering around the airport, not knowing what had happened and not knowing when the flight would be rescheduled."

Kenny enjoyed the trip, even though the confusion surrounding the first leg of the flight because of the dense fog was unsettling.

"That recruiting visit to Nebraska was the first time I ever flew on a plane," Kenny said. "We got to Lincoln, and it was the coldest day of my life, even worse than the coldest day I had ever experienced in Colorado. Coach Tenopir showed up to meet Coach White and me, and Coach Tenopir wasn't even wearing a jacket, just a thin shirt. A sign said the temperature was below freezing. I said, 'Coach Tenopir, is it always freezing?' He said, 'It's not always this cold, but it is cold here for a lot of the year.' "

"We went to the football offices and stopped at the Cornhusker Hotel," Walker said. "We met Coach Osborne when we toured Nebraska's football offices. I looked at all the trophies, and then they took me to Coach Osborne's office. I forgot about everything when I saw the fish on his wall. We started talking about fishing, and I could tell that we both shared a love for it. We didn't talk about football. We talked about school."

"Coach Osborne, I will need someone to interpret for class and for football meetings," Walker said.

"Well, we'll certainly have someone available, since we really need to have that to make it work," Osborne said.

That "someone" ended up being a person who would change Kenny's life—Mimi Mann.

"When Kenny first showed up, I had no idea if this would be a lasting relationship—I didn't even know if he would pick Nebraska," Mann said. "I didn't know anything about recruiting or football— almost nothing in the world about either. My understanding was that I was going to be there interpreting one day, and that was it."

While the interpreter wasn't the only reason Walker chose Nebraska, it did play a major part.

"One thing that turned Kenny on to Nebraska was that they have a hearing-impaired program at Nebraska that was federally funded," White said. "When we went up there for our visit, Mimi was there. She went everywhere with us during the recruiting visit.

That was the only school that did that. They told him she'd be with him from now on. That was important."

For Mann, the biggest adjustment was learning something—anything—about football.

"I was so far detached from sports that—if you can believe this—I didn't even know where South Stadium was," Mann said, "so I had to go the day before the meeting just to make sure I didn't get lost and wasn't late."

While working with a major college football program was new, Mann was used to unique situations. In fact, much of her work as an interpreter is for things out of the norm.

"I was on autopilot and did things by the book, which you are supposed to do in situations you are unsure of," Mann said. "I was used to being in situations for unusual things, like sex therapy for deaf people, transients who were deaf, all sorts of things. Yet, this college football world was one about which I had no idea."

While Mann was on "autopilot," she admits Kenny's personality was as special as his situation.

"I thought he was a really, really nice guy," Mann said. "The first day when he came for his recruiting visit, I was thinking, 'Well, if UNL wants him, I hope he comes for UNL's sake because he has some sort of talent or something.' But aside from that, I didn't have many thoughts at first about the whole thing."

Kenny also had a perspective and attitude that not many other recruits seemed to possess.

"All the freshmen around him came in sort of cocky—but he didn't seem to be that way," Mann said. "I think I sensed a relief in him that he could communicate here. None of the other colleges recruiting him hired an interpreter."

Mann thought Nebraska would be fortunate if it was able to land Walker, but her reasoning had nothing to do with football.

"I just thought he was a really nice guy, and I could care less about the sports part of it," Mann said. "This was all pretty ho-hum to me, as opposed to how my husband would have dealt with it; I remember thinking, 'Boy, my husband would give his right arm to do this.' But I was just doing my job."

Mann said Walker's sign language skills were rough, especially at first.

"Kenny is difficult to interpret for because his signs are not gorgeous," Mann said. "He was the only deaf person in the whole county when he lived in Crane, so he didn't get a lot of practice, much less the proper practice. Since he only worked with an interpreter once a month, it was difficult for him to build on the skill and keep it up."

Mann got an idea how talented of an athlete Walker was when strength coach Boyd Epley happened upon them.

"We were in the weight room, and Kenny was playing with the weights," Mann said. "Kenny did a vertical jump, and Boyd said, 'Wow, we have some stallion horses coming today, but this one is the studdest of the studs.' I thought, 'Oh, maybe they do want him. I hope he picks UNL.' It was interesting to see all of these things because I really was so far out of my element. Now if I was interpreting at a jewelry store, I could have really gotten into it."

While it was apparent she could—if called upon—work with Walker if he ended up in Lincoln, Mann had no idea what the future held.

"We got along real well and everything, but like I said, it was just business on my end," Mann said. "Maybe it was in the stars for something to turn out very special. But right away? No, I did not sense that."

Walker said he felt good about the Nebraska visit from the time he arrived in chilly Lincoln. However, he said meeting Mann put Nebraska No. 1 on his list—by a mile.

"I felt so good meeting Mimi," Kenny said. "When I met Mimi, I knew I was coming to Nebraska. Words can't describe my experience. Finally, I had someone who understood me, who new what I had to do to be successful, and Coach Osborne was so supportive. He said, 'If it is something we need to do, within NCAA and school rules, we will do it because we want all of our students to be successful.' Coach Osborne was very clear about what it was going to be like for me at Nebraska."

Walker kept waiting to find fault in something about Nebraska. Yet, at every turn, he was more and more impressed.

"We went to the stadium, and he showed me all the facilities," Kenny said. "I looked around at everything, and it was just incredible. Everything—and everyone—was so nice. I could see the dining room, and they had lots of food on the table. Coach Osborne, Mimi, the strong academic program—everything I wanted and needed was there."

Mann could tell that Coach White, while excited about the opportunities Kenny found waiting at Nebraska, still felt a little trepidation.

"Rickey kind of reached out to me," Mann said. "I could tell that Kenny felt very close to him, that Coach White had been a father figure to him. I had a sense that Rickey was torn, like 'I am going to lose him, and I hope this is good for him.' I felt a sense of vulnerability. My husband had coached, and he would get sad when his players moved on. I could tell that was how Rickey felt. I could tell Rickey and Kenny were good friends."

White said Mann's perception was correct.

"Even though Mimi was professional, I could see from how she handled herself that she was a very caring, sensitive person," White said. "And I will be honest with you, that really helped put me at ease."

While Mann did all she could to keep the relationship businesslike, she admits that something special did happen that afternoon as the day wound down and Kenny and Coach White were getting ready to leave.

"Rickey said he wanted to get something that said Nebraska on it, but that he didn't have much time," Mann said. "I told him about the Husker shop right across the street from the stadium. He started off on a run because time was short. I had heard about NCAA rules and that kind of thing, but nothing specifically, so I didn't know what I could say to Kenny before he left."

Mann kept it simple and short.

"Good-bye," Mann told Kenny as they stood in the area known as South Stadium, within the walls of Memorial Stadium.

Having heard her husband talk about the hallowed turf at Memorial Stadium, Mann decided to take a peek at the field.

"I thought, 'Jim makes such a big deal about this stadium and how awe-inspiring it is, so I am going to grab the gusto and walk across this turf to see what it feels like,' " Mann said. "I had no reason to believe that day would not be my only opportunity to do that. I took a few steps out onto the field and noticed it was kind of spongy and felt funny. Suddenly, I felt this presence behind me, coming very close. I turned and saw only the outline of Kenny. He is so big and dark-skinned that all I could make out was his silhouette because the sun over his head was almost blinding. But what I will never forget is how the sun looked like a kind of halo over Kenny's head—that really struck me."

Walker made eye contact with Mann.

"I will never forget you," Kenny told her.

Mann used sign language to tell Kenny, "What you've just said, I agree with. I won't forget you, either."

"I felt weak in the knees," Mann said. "It was just so touching. Here's this guy who should be cocky on a recruiting visit to a big-time school, and his so-called 'stud appeal' must have been dampened by having this old lady waddling around with him. It just struck me that he came back. I thought, 'Oh my gosh, what just happened?' "

Kenny knew what just happened: he became a Husker.

"I told my family as soon as I got home that I was going to Nebraska," Kenny said. "I told them I didn't care if I had to live 18 hours away from home, that my heart would be warm and safe in Nebraska. My family all looked at me as though I was crazy."

Mann and Coach Osborne were a perfect fit for Walker, who left feeling as good about his potential off the field as he did on it.

"It's more than just football to Coach Osborne," Walker said. "He cares about the players, about more than football. The players are like his family. He has a lot of concern about their lives, how they do in school. It's like he was the best coach and person you could ever hope for. We had so many walk-on players through the years. I remember all the ones who never got into games, but he knew who they were, even if they didn't play. He cared about them all the same—that was amazing to me. He told us to work hard in the classroom. It's hard for other people to understand. I thought you just had to be a good player to make it at Nebraska. But that's only part of it. They don't look down on a single player in that program."

Walker's other recruiting visits were far less memorable.

"The other coaches had egos," Kenny said. "I remember I asked Barry Switzer if he had an interpreter. He said, 'An interpreter, for what?' He didn't know anything about that. I don't fault him for that, but for me to go on and see how Nebraska handled it made me really feel fortunate to have met Coach Osborne and the rest of the staff."

Mann, adhering strictly to the letter of the interpreter's ethics, did not discuss her day with her husband Jim, even though she was dying inside to tell him.

"Jim was at a church meeting when I got done," Mann said. "I was missing it, so I rushed back and sat in the meeting with him. First of all, I don't know if my husband would have even believed me had I told him about my day, and that I walked on the field that he had spoken of so much. More importantly, as an interpreter you can never tell anyone what you do during your work day because that makes you a part of your client's life and his/her experience. I was there to be nothing more than a communication device—a telephone, if you will. Before television became a part of society, the deaf community did everything together. If you said something to someone deaf, they would share it with all of their friends because all they really had was each other. So for an interpreter to talk about his/her work is professional suicide—you just can't tell anyone anything."

CHAPTER 5

PROUD TO BE A HUSKER

The trauma of leaving the friendly confines of Crane was buoyed by the fact that people like Mimi Mann and Tom Osborne were in Lincoln. While Walker knew his life was changing dramatically, Mann was still unsure of the impact her connection to Walker was going to have on every aspect of her life.

"When Kenny did sign with Nebraska, I was asked to come down there," Mann said. "I went in, again on autopilot. I gave my little speech about being just a communication device to Coach Tony Samuel, who was Kenny's position coach when Kenny was playing linebacker at first. I told him, 'Coach Samuel, I'm an interpreter. Everything you say, I will sign—everything. Just consider me a telephone line to bridge communication. No one else will know what is said between us, except Kenny. So speak like you always speak. If you curse, I will sign that, too.' "

Keeping a professional distance remained a goal of Mann's.

"When I was on autopilot, I could not be a person or a friend," Mann said. "You aren't there to be their momma—you are not there to love and support them, and you aren't there to advise them. You are there to open up communication, period. You run big risks if you do anything more. You can get too close to them, and then that puts them in more of a handicapped position because they depend too much on you, and that in itself can be worse than the deafness. So I was thinking about that constantly."

Although Mann knew the reverence with which Husker fans hold their team, she didn't think the long arm of the media would come crashing in on her working relationship with Walker.

"I thought this would be a very professional situation," Mann said. "A couple of times, I had been involved with a deaf person who was well regarded and known by the media. Tony knew the media would come in, but I didn't. Sure enough, we go outside, and the media is swarming. They swarmed right to me. I was thinking, 'Now, how am I going to protect his confidentiality?' "

Mann came up with a plan.

"I won't give my name," Mann told herself. "I did that before, and it worked out great. They took a photo of a person I was signing for, and even though my back made it into the paper, it just said 'So and so's interpreter.' That is how I wanted it because I knew I had an obligation to the deaf community to not be a part of the story."

No problem, Mann thought, just step by step, one, two, three. Wrong, wrong, wrong.

"We go out to face the media, and someone said, 'Mimi,' so they already knew my name," Mann said. "The sports information office had given it to them. I didn't even know that Nebraska had a sports information office, and I didn't know such a thing existed or what they did to that point. I thought, 'Oh no, my professional life is out the window! Everything is wrong. This is ruining everything.' "

The world she had known and the reputation she had built professionally were teetering on the edge of a cliff. She could either reel herself back in and try to duck the press, or she and Walker could find a way to salvage some positive out of all the attention coming their way.

"That came to be the most all-pervasive thing in my life for the next five years," Mann said. "I wanted to be professional and obey the ethics, but the media was asking me questions that I couldn't answer."

So Mann pulled Walker aside.

"Kenny," Mann said, "I don't know how to handle this and protect your confidentiality."

Walker responded.

"Let's use this to create awareness for the deaf community," Walker told her. "This is a chance to help people understand what it's like to be deaf and the challenges deaf people face."

"Are you positive?" Mann signed to Kenny. "Because if we do this today, there is no turning back."

"Let's do it," Kenny answered.

"In the long run," Mann says looking back, "it worked out well."

Things weren't going as well for Kenny. His first roommate liked to party.

"It was hard for me when I first started at Nebraska," Walker said. "I lived alone after my roommate got kicked out of the dorm for unacceptable behavior—he did a lot of partying. The second kid I roomed with, a quiet, nice kid who was a walk-on on the football team, was from Nebraska. Two weeks after we started living together, he moved to another dorm to be closer to his girlfriend. After that happened, my dorm supervisor said I could have a room alone. I liked it, but it was lonely at times."

He was able to communicate well with his teammates, especially with having Mann's talents to help ease him into new relationships.

"It wasn't hard to communicate," Kenny said. "We would talk and work out together. As we got to know each other, it would increase our communication more and more."

The coach who recruited Walker to Nebraska, Milt Tenopir, used Kenny's deafness to his advantage.

"I remember Kenny's first year at Nebraska," Tenopir said. "One of my jobs was to call defenses for the scout team, which Kenny was on at the time. As we got going, I realized how well Kenny read lips. So I would stand back behind the offense and mouth the offense to Kenny, and no one else knew I was doing this. Kenny would turn around and call the defense. Now, that part of it is kind of funny. But what you have to understand is that Kenny really understood the game. It was a pleasure to have him around."

Mann said she and Walker put together a whole new verse of sign language—of the gridiron variety—to deal with the terminology the coaches used.

"We ended up inventing about 500 signs," Mann said. "I could never get a substitute interpreter because there were no signs for 80 percent of the phrases the coaches told me, so Kenny and I developed our own language.

"After that first meeting with Tony Samuel, I said, 'I can't do this. I'm not doing this right. I'm spelling out every single word. I know he's not getting what you're telling him because I'm not getting it myself,' " Mann said. "But the coaches were great. After every meeting, they'd take time to explain everything to me I didn't understand. We changed a lot of signs, making Kenny be the upright index finger, and I'd show him what the coaches wanted. It went much quicker and made sense to Kenny, but as far as what the football jargon meant? I had no clue."

"Dog the three gap," Coach Samuel said, "then you have the nose guard."

"What is a nose guard?" Mann asked Samuel.

Samuel drew circles and squares on the board, and pointed to one.

"That's the nose guard," Samuel said, pointing to one.

"Why are some circles, and others are squares?" Mann asked. "Is that how few people there are? Only 11 on a team at a time?"

"That's how basic they had to go over it for me," Mann said. "I certainly wouldn't say I could be a coach now, but I do understand the game to where my husband really likes watching football with me. On the other hand, if the coaches would have used opals and diamonds instead of squares and circles, they would have really had my attention."

Mann did all she could to stay out of the way in an effort to make both Kenny's and the coaches' jobs easier.

"Especially at first I kept the attitude that I couldn't become friends with these people—his coaches and teammates—because if I got to be buddies with them, the other players and coaches might establish relationships with me, instead of Kenny," Mann said. "So I focused on coming across as an interpreter who was aloof and cold, even though that's pretty much not how I am as a person."

On the field Kenny found a spot on the freshman team. While the freshman team no longer exists at Nebraska, it helped Kenny make the adjustment go smoother than it might have had he been buried deep on the depth chart that season.

"One of the players the first week had a chance to hit me, but let up and changed directions," Kenny said. "I asked him what he was doing. He said, 'Kenny, I was afraid to hit you because you are deaf.' I said, 'Hit me as hard as you can. I am ready for it.' "

Kenny felt he was ready for whatever lay ahead. He was wrong.

"I was lucky to be moved up to the varsity my freshman year after I led the freshman team in sacks," Kenny said. "Still, it seemed like during my freshman year, I was not that serious about football. The coaches encouraged me to try harder to reach my potential. The first day at varsity football it was a big change, an altogether different perspective."

The freshman team was a world apart from the potent Husker varsity squad.

"The freshman team was a good experience," Kenny said, "but it was like half-speed compared to the varsity. It was embarrassing practicing with the varsity because by the time I'd get to the quarterback, he'd no longer have the football. So I'd look for the running back, and he'd be all the way down the field. I felt so slow."

That was quite a turnaround from his initial experience.

"On the freshman team, I felt like I had an 'S' on my shirt—I was Superman," Kenny said.

Superman found Kryptonite in the form of the Husker varsity.

"I was practicing against the varsity," Kenny said, "and I broke free through the gap, and what happened was the I-back—the third string I-back—John Kelly, had run full speed through my chest and knocked me down on the field. He was running and running down the field, and I was on my back. I thought, 'Oh man, what hit me?' "

The second healthy dose of humility was just one block away.

"The next play, Kevin Lighter, an offensive guard who pulled on the play, just ran me over," Kenny said. "I got up, and I couldn't see out of one of my eyes—I thought I had lost one of my eyes. It turned out I was hit so hard that my helmet was turned all the way around, and I was looking out of the earhole. Coach Tenopir said, 'Get your butt up. Let's go!' I was thinking, 'Wow, what happened?' On the freshman team, I could blow over the fullback like he was paper. Not on the varsity."

Another helping of humble pie was on the way a few plays later.

"I grabbed the fullback by his shirt to pull him down, and it ripped the skin off my fingers," Kenny said. "It even hurt my chest. I came into the locker room after practice, and I was not happy. I took off my shoulder pads, and they were broken. The next day, I broke a second set of shoulder pads. I borrowed another pair the next day, and broke those.

"So through the first three days, I broke three sets of shoulder pads, lost the skin off my fingers, thought I was blinded because my helmet was knocked around my head and was just altogether very sore, a soreness I had never felt before," Kenny said.

His freshman year ended on what Kenny believed to be a high note. But that was not the case. Even though he made big strides, Walker was not going to be able to play linebacker at Nebraska because of communication problems.

Walker's second year was almost his last at Nebraska. No longer able to star on the freshman team, Walker was not one of the top players at the varsity level. He redshirted his second year, meaning he would be a sophomore the following season. However, redshirting meant Walker could not play in any games for the Huskers.

"I was making too many mistakes playing outside linebacker, so I was getting downgraded, and it didn't look like I was ever going to play," Kenny said. "I wasn't grading out high enough to be a starter. I wasn't very happy. Coach McBride asked me if I wanted to move to defensive end."

Kenny remembers the day as if it were yesterday.

"I had experience working with deaf players when I was in Wisconsin," McBride said. "Would you like to try to be a defensive lineman?"

Walker said sure, he'd give it a go.

"I weighed only 230 pounds," Walker said, "but that was the last hope for me because it was obvious I wasn't going to work out at any other position."

McBride thought the move was logical for Walker.

"After watching Kenny go through what he did playing linebacker," McBride said, "I thought he was big enough and strong enough to play on the defensive line. He had to make fewer adjustments there than at linebacker. We were fortunate because we had Pat Englebert at nose tackle, and he and Kenny communicated with each other really well. If there was an adjustment or we changed defenses, Pat would give Kenny a hand signal."

Walker's high school coach at Crane, Rickey White, said McBride's action showed that Nebraska would do whatever it took for any student-athlete in any situation.

"I was wishing that he could end up doing well at Nebraska," White said. "We all knew that Kenny was a very intelligent person and he had athletic ability. I just didn't know if his handicap would prevent him from succeeding at such a high level. When he first arrived at Nebraska, he struggled, but he never gave up. The coaches at Nebraska care about the kids so much it's amazing. They did everything they could to help Kenny be successful."

Coach McBride, for the first time, had seen signs of quitting in Walker in the days leading up to when McBride suggested the position switch.

"It had gotten to the point where Kenny might have been ready to give up because he didn't feel like he could learn anything more to increase his chance of playing linebacker," McBride said. "Yet, he came back from that setback and became not just a player, not just a starter, but an All-American—one of the top players in the country."

But initially, the transition was far from complete. Walker's heart was not in his new position.

"Kenny's life at Nebraska wasn't tied up with a pretty bow and placed in front of him, and his sophomore year was his worst," Mann said. "We almost lost him. The coaches wanted to redshirt him because he had switched positions so many times. He had done all this work, and this was something Kenny thought might mean the beginning of the end for him because it would take him out of the program in some ways for the entire season. He had done all of this work. And he wasn't having fun. His classes were even more challenging."

Unable to motivate himself for the first time in his life, Walker was speeding downhill. It looked like neither football nor school was going to work out. All the long hours and dreams were fading to but a memory, until Mann stepped in.

She felt like she had to intervene because not only was Kenny wasting his time, he was wasting her time, too.

"It was looking like a long, long year," Mann said. "For the first time, Kenny gave up. We had to be very cruel to him. One weekend he wanted to come over. So I was going to confront him and give him the what-for. He had been sleeping in meetings, and I kept signing. I knew my hands were going to run out—I was starting to get carpal tunnel syndrome—and I knew I was wasting my hands signing while he was sleeping. Kenny wasn't taking advantage of all the resources he had."

Knowing Kenny—like any other 20-year-old in the same circumstances—might not want to confront the situation, Mann invited him over to the house.

"We went in the backyard, and Jon Crippen, a teammate and roommate who had brought Kenny over, went to get gas and would be gone for a while so Kenny couldn't get up and leave when I made him mad," Mann said.

Mann realized at that point that it was going to have to be a tough love kind of thing.

"You aren't trying," Mann told him. "Would you rather go back to Texas?"

"I don't know what I want," Kenny said. "I can't decide."

Walker looked away, and Mann drew his attention back to her as she signed furiously.

"This is the decision you are making—your indecision is your decision," Mann said. "You are not going to class. You are flunking. If you don't go to class, you will not play. If you flunk out, they will not keep you here."

Kenny again looked away, choosing to stare off into the distance rather than watch Mann sign the truth to him. Mann knew Walker had worked in the summertime mowing lawns in Crane, so she used that as an ace up her sleeve to bring home the perspective of what was at stake.

"You have two options," Mann told him. "You can stay here and get a degree, or go back to Crane and mow lawns the rest of your life. Coach McBride is doing as much as any human could ever do for another man, and you are wasting it. Save him the grief and go home now."

Walker looked in every direction. Coming to Nebraska was supposed to be the answer, yet he had more questions than he had when he arrived.

"He started crying, really crying," Mann said. "He looked like a lamb to slaughter. I put my arm around him, and he recoiled, kind of melted back and hunched over."

"Where is Jon?" Kenny asked.

"Jon's not here," Mann told him.

Walker went into Mann's bathroom, splashed some cold water on his face, and made himself a promise.

"I took a long look at myself in the mirror and said, 'That's it. It's time to get serious,'" Kenny said.

The change in attitude was immediate, although Walker had a lot of leg work to do to make up the time he had slacked off academically. He finished out the year and came back for his third year, but since he redshirted the previous year, it meant he was only a sophomore when it came to eligibility.

"He really started working out hard," Mann said. "And he saw immediate gains in the weight room. He started doing better in class, but that did take a little more time. With working out, you can lift a lot of weight in a short time and see the results relatively quickly. In class, you don't see the results as quickly. But Kenny put on a lot of muscle, started paying attention in meetings and then had his head on completely straight heading into his junior year."

The criticism from the coaches was taken better, too.

"The coaches got on me, but they just wanted me to get better, and I really picked up on that," Kenny said. "I hit the weights hard and started to get stronger very quickly. Just the lifting itself made me feel better and more confident. A few weeks later, I stopped getting run over. I wasn't scared anymore. I was tired of getting beaten, so I started dishing out the beatings."

Under the guidance of McBride, Walker found out that he was as talented as the other defensive linemen. All he lacked was experience and technique.

"Those other defensive linemen were just so big and so physical," Kenny said. "Yet, defense seemed more fun because the calls were easier. But it is different. You have a lot of information you need to pick up. I liked linebacker because you have to be very aggressive. So I used that aggression on the defensive line."

A nagging ankle injury kept Walker frustrated because he could not play. But he got his chance to show what he could do during the final game of the season. And as it turned out, that game changed Walker's standing as a Husker.

"I didn't play as a sophomore until the bowl game against Miami," Kenny said. "I hurt my ankle against UCLA, and that slowed me down during the entire season. I wasn't even expected to play against Miami. Coach McBride forced me to go out on the field because they needed someone."

Walker pleaded with McBride not to send him into the game because he was afraid he would fail.

"I told them I wasn't sure if I was ready because I hadn't played all year and the ankle was sore, even though the doctors said it had healed," Kenny said.

Being afraid to fail is a sure ticket out of a top-notch program like Nebraska. So McBride made the decision for Walker.

"It doesn't matter whether you are 100 percent or not," McBride said, "you have to go out there."

McBride's expertise and intuitiveness saved Walker's career and put his motivation at an all-time high heading into spring football the following year.

"That day, everything in football changed for me—it was just amazing," Walker said. "I had no trouble with Miami's offensive linemen. I thought to myself, 'My gosh, you guys aren't stronger than me. Why are our defensive linemen struggling with them?' The Miami players were strong and quick, but that was what I was, too. So I learned from that, that you could be quicker and faster. That night I found out I could do something to help us—use my speed on the pass rush."

He finished his sophomore year with two unassisted tackles and one assisted tackle. Hardly numbers to hang one's hat on—yet, that was just a fraction of the huge numbers Walker would post in the following two years.

Looking back, Walker knows things worked out nearly perfectly. However, he also knows that without McBride and Mann, he could have been back home in a heartbeat.

"It worked out real good for me," Walker said. "The next year, my junior year, was a big change. I was starting to become a star because I could get up the field really quickly and into the other team's backfield."

Walker started getting his coach's attention and that of his teammates as well that spring. Osborne was relieved to see Walker start to make his mark in the classroom, as well as on the field, after the period of struggle.

"We probably didn't realize at the time how many steps we would have to go through to make it work—we didn't realize what it would take," Osborne said. "We thought that defensively we could just turn him loose, and he could play. But there's a lot of complexity on defense. So it was a little more work on the field than perhaps we anticipated. Off the field, it was about what we thought. He made up for it with his attitude and work ethic."

CHAPTER 6

LIFE IN LINCOLN

When Kenny first showed up in Lincoln, he was, like all other freshmen, put into the dorm with his other first-year teammates. Jon Crippen and Morgan Gregory met Walker the first day. The trio roomed together during the grueling summer two-a-day practices as the student-athletes reported three weeks before school started.

"I remember we had the corner room in the dorm—right next to the train tracks," Crippen said. "During two-a-day practices, we were more exhausted than anyone could ever imagine. That first night—and the nights that followed—we heard the trains going by twice an hour, sometimes more than that, all night long. Morgan and I were putting pillows on our heads to try and do anything to muffle all that noise."

Across the room, their roommate slept like a baby.

"Didn't hear a thing," Kenny said. "Remember? I am deaf."

Not only did Crippen and Gregory have to get up exhausted, they had to rustle Kenny.

"We'd have to wake Kenny up in the morning because he slept so soundly," Crippen said. "Morgan and I were really dragging from the practices and the lack of sleep. Not Kenny. He was up and raring to go. He thought that was pretty funny. That's where our relationship started. And it just grew from there."

While the coaching staff had legitimate concerns about communicating with Walker, Crippen said after the first day, communicating with and understanding Kenny grew easier.

"There are all kinds of ways to communicate, verbally and non-verbally," Crippen said. "You think to yourself, 'This guy is deaf; how will we talk?' But he talks and talks—and talks some more because he really likes to communicate—and eventually, you get to understand him. People say, 'How can you understand each other?

You don't know sign language.' But we had our own language. Kenny would talk, and he knew our mannerisms and could read lips. So it wasn't the kind of problem people would think. We communicated very well."

That the three were randomly thrown together ended up benefiting each one, as well as expanding each's world.

"We just hit it off," Crippen said. "We grew up in three different worlds. I was from a big town in the South, Houston. Morgan was from the Midwest, Denver. And Kenny was from a small town in Texas, Crane. We were away from home for the first time, looking to identify with someone else. And here we were, in what we, at that time, believed to be the middle of nowhere. It just happened to work out where we had three different personalities, but we all meshed."

While Walker faced the greatest challenge when it came to communicating, it was Crippen and Gregory who were quiet.

"It's ironic that people think Kenny is shy because he is deaf," Crippen said. "Because the truth is that Kenny's the type of person who is very outgoing and loves to meet new people. Morgan and I, if you meet us for the first time, are much more introverted. Kenny really helped us as far as meeting people."

When football camp ended, the players were assigned new rooms.

"After we roomed together for fall football camp, which was about three weeks, Morgan and I got a dorm room together when school started, and Kenny had his own room," Crippen said. "But really, we were still all roommates even then because either Morgan and I were over at Kenny's room, or he was at our room. And it wasn't just us three—Kenny had a lot of friends on the team, probably more than a lot of guys had."

Once they quickly figured out that Kenny was just like any other student-athlete, the guys started acting like any other college kids.

"Morgan was kind of a jokester," Crippen said. "It's hard to talk about because it sounds like we were cruel. But it's just like if you have a short friend, and after you get close, you can make short jokes. You see, Kenny could laugh at his impairment. We would do things that people would think—just upon hearing them out of context—were cruel. But believe me, Kenny did more than his share of things and more than held his own. We'd do things like plan something because he couldn't hear us. He'd sense it or pick up on our body language and do things right back, which left him with the upper hand of a joke that Morgan and I had planned. He'd catch me and Morgan—we'd think, 'He doesn't know what we're talking about; he won't know.' And then Kenny would turn around and say, 'I know what you're doing; you'll get hurt.' "

Since Crippen and Gregory were able to meet Mimi Mann through her association with Kenny, an extended family was born.

"We would see Mimi a lot, going to her house and that kind of thing," Crippen said. "Their family had open arms to us three. That kept us together, too. We would go there on the weekend, which gave us somewhere to go, a family to talk to. I consider Mimi a second family to me, and I think Kenny and Morgan would say the same thing. And Kenny, Morgan and I—well, we were just like brothers."

Mann realized during the first week of two-a-day practices that Kenny would need more than just a good interpreter to survive the initial shock of his new surroundings and routine.

"NCAA rules were very restrictive and did not permit Kenny to be a frequent visitor in our home," Mann said. "But I knew he needed it. The coaches didn't call me and tell me to invite him over. They just called and said, 'He is crying on the field.' I knew I had to do something. I didn't care if we lost Kenny Walker, the football player, but as a mother I didn't want to see Kenny Walker, the person, leave the school too early and for the wrong reasons. It was his first week here, and I thought all he needed was to see a family, a dog and a backyard, and to be around someone who can communicate with him."

Mann and her family never viewed Kenny and his friends as an obligation. Rather, it was an opportunity for both sides to see another world.

"My first motherly feeling was to my two daughters because I saw what an emotionally enriching experience this could be, to have athletes who are black and from other areas come into their lives," Mann said. "That was one of the first reasons I was thrilled to have them over—even forgetting the fact they were really neat guys. All of this just evolved. It all fell into place like this."

The various members of the extended "family" helped each other develop their weaknesses into strengths as they shared common interests and learned about each other by discovering their differences.

"It was just that way," Mann said. "Everybody in his/her own way did things together; Kenny with the girls; Jon or Morgan with them or my husband; Kenny and my husband talking for hours; Jon and Kenny fishing; Morgan kidding around with the girls. It was like an extended family, and everyone did things together and endeared themselves to each other. It wasn't like they were my friends, or even they were just friends because it really did grow to be like a family."

And "this place"—the Manns' home in Lincoln—would never be the same again.

"All we gave those guys was a place to come and chill, to get away from the pressures," Mann said. "We thoroughly enjoyed having them over. They used to love to watch the fights on television. I didn't care about that. But they'd sit there and predict who was going to win, and they'd get going pretty good watching the fight. Now, wouldn't you know it; our daughters are boxing fans. These guys drew them into all these sports they probably would have never learned about otherwise."

Despite the fact that Mann's long hours took time away from her family, she said her husband and children enjoyed the experience as much as she did—and offered unconditional support.

"Nebraska played in the Japan Bowl, so I was gone from home for days and days," Mann said. "Someone asked me, 'Doesn't your family resent this, all the time you are away?' That just never occurred in my family. My husband and children saw that Kenny had a need for something I could provide. So they didn't have a qualm with me providing it. And my girls would do anything they could to help the guys not feel homesick. It was a give-and-get situation for everyone involved."

While her son was in an unfamiliar town more than 1,000 miles away from the friendly confines of Crane, Julia Walker felt quite at ease.

"I loved the University of Nebraska," Julia said, "but I really only spoke with Coach Osborne maybe once. I didn't really have any need to be constantly communicating with him. But I did hear a lot about Coach Osborne from Kenny and others who knew Coach. Mimi told me what a good Christian man Coach Osborne was, so that right there really put my mind at ease as far as not worrying about Kenny's welfare in Lincoln, especially having someone as special as Mimi Mann and her family there."

While the NCAA rules might have frowned on what the Manns were doing, Mimi said she and her family provided only emotional support.

"We weren't in a financial position to give him anything like a car," Mann said, "and we weren't the kind who were going to cook big steaks for him because we couldn't afford that, either. We might have been breaking rules to have him over to the house. But we were just being human beings—and that should never be against any rules."

The menu was simple—no porterhouses or delicacies—but the company was what Crippen, Gregory and Walker showed up for each time.

"We'd sit around and have hamburgers and hot dogs, bread and macaroni," Mann said. "All three of those boys had big appetites. If we'd have picked more expensive food, we'd have gone broke."

What Walker was hungry for was not so much food, but communication.

"Kenny was starved for information," Mann said. "Deaf people will say this universally: they never feel as lonely as they do when they are sitting at a meal with others. Someone will say something like, 'This lady down the road was hit by a car.' Everyone else will be like, 'What? Where? When?' All this conversation takes place, and the deaf person is completely out of the loop. By the time he's able to say, 'What happened?' someone will just say, 'Susie was hit by a car. She's fine now.' Here they had this intense conversation for several minutes that everyone was wrapped up in, and the deaf person gets it later in two short sentences. So the deaf person feels left out and misses all the details."

Mimi's husband and Kenny spent a lot of quality time together, especially around the dinner table.

"Kenny used to love to sit and talk to my husband Jim about

current events," Mann said. "When my husband had his mustache trimmed real well, Kenny could read his lips really good. So one night they were talking about the Arabs and the Israelis, and Kenny wanted to understand why they can't get along. Jim was going on and on, repeating himself, and Kenny just wasn't getting it. So they called me in. What happened was the words 'Jews' and 'shoes' look exactly alike to a lip reader."

So, obviously, Kenny knew the problem went deeper than footwear.

"We would sit at the table for two to three hours, laughing about things that went on," Mann said. "Kenny would say something at his own expense, and Morgan would climb right on that."

The stories kept Mann's family in stitches.

"One time the night before they came over, they had been arguing over what TV channel to watch. Kenny had gotten mad and thrown something that broke the aquarium at their place," Mann said. "They egged each other on the whole night."

Another time involved Kenny's activities at a party the night before.

"Kenny was eating dinner, and Morgan started talking about a party they had been to the night before," Mann said. "Kenny read Morgan's lips, and said, 'No more, that's enough. Don't tell them that!' Morgan said, 'Come on Kenny, tell the Manns what you did last night.' Kenny had kissed a girl who was not very attractive. Morgan said, 'He kissed her right on the lips. That Kenny, he's the Kissing Sasquatch.' Kenny said, 'You fool! You fool!' Morgan said, 'You're the fool—I wasn't the one kissing the ugly girl!' They were just hysterical."

Walker still rolls his eyes when asked about that night.

"Those guys," Walker said, "didn't let me forget about that for a long time."

Mann said it wasn't always as much fun for Kenny during his freshman year. "I knew it was often difficult for Kenny to adjust to college life. But I saw someone who was suffering. As a mother, when you see someone suffering who doesn't have friends yet, you will do something. We gave him no car and no cash. We just invited him to our home occasionally. Most college players leave home, and it is tough. Throw in the deafness and the distance in Kenny's case, and you could see where he was experiencing the feelings that any young man in his position would feel."

Walker's warmth and sensitivity was matched by a sense of perceptiveness that endeared Kenny even more to Mimi.

"Kenny is a very intuitive person, and he reads expressions and body language very well," Mann said. "Kenny was friends with my husband's father. Jim, Kenny and Jim's father would do things together sometimes. Well, Jim's father had open heart surgery, and apparently I was wearing a look of concern on my face that day when I showed up at the campus. Right when I approached him, Kenny said, 'What's wrong?' He persisted and I told him, and Kenny expressed his concern and wanted to know what he could do to help. That's just the kind of person Kenny is and a big part of what makes him so special."

The time with Kenny, Crippen and Gregory is a time the Manns still cherish.

"That's one of the greatest gifts I ever gave to my husband— three sons," Mimi said. "And I gave my daughters three big brothers. The guys always felt very responsible and protective of my daughters. When Kenny visited and found out Darcy was very serious about the guy she ended up marrying, he made the guy come over and pass his test. So Kenny and those guys were just a wonderful gift for our family."

Walker, Mann said, enjoyed the times he had carving his own path, especially in social situations.

"Kenny established incredible relationships without any help from me—like when I wasn't around," Mann said.

Mann said she often watched with a smile from across a room as Walker made his friends laugh.

"Anybody who spent more than five minutes around him picked up on his sense of humor, whether I was there or not," Mann said.

Kenny's mother, Julia, said Kenny made the most of his time at Nebraska, which was aided by his relationship with people like Tom Osborne and Mimi Mann.

"People talk a lot about student-athletes not fulfilling their potential," Julia said. "But for his time at Nebraska, Kenny could not have done any better. I have to give all the credit for that to Mimi.

She took Kenny into her home with her two little girls and Jim, her husband. They were just wonderful to Kenny. When I was going through a struggling period, they helped Kenny with food and that kind of thing, inviting him to eat at their house."

Crippen and Kenny grew especially close, and when they weren't studying, playing football or hanging out at the Manns' house, the two would go fishing. Crippen has enough fishing stories to last a lifetime.

"This is the night I will never forget," Crippen said. "We used to go fishing after practice. After Friday practices during spring ball, we'd go to the lake and take sandwiches and stuff. We'd sit out there all night. At night, of course, you can't see your fishing line very well. So you put a bell on your pole, so you'll hear it when you get a nibble. Well, Kenny put a bell on his pole when it got dark. I was like, 'You are deaf; why do you have a bell?' He said, "Look, it is shiny, and it moves, shifting the light.' I said, 'OK, that makes sense.' You don't think of those things if you can hear. Yet, once you think about it, it makes sense. He used the same tool—the bell—for the same reason, but he just used a different means to the same end.

"Well, it got later and later, and real dark," Crippen said. "We heard something right behind us—I heard it, and Kenny felt the movement of the weeds rustling—it just scared us both to death. Kenny shines a light, and it's an animal. I could tell right away that it was a skunk, but Kenny thought it was something else, like something that might attack us because it didn't run away. I grew up on a farm, so I knew we didn't want to scare the skunk. Kenny was thinking about our safety, still not realizing it was a skunk, so he picked up a rock. 'I'll take care of it!' he yelled. I said, 'No Kenny, it's a skunk! It will spray us.' Kenny wasn't looking at me, so he couldn't read my lips and didn't know what I was saying. I'm a small guy compared to Kenny, who was about 6-4, 245 pounds at that time. Since Kenny couldn't hear me, I had to do something. Kenny raised his arm to throw the rock, and I jumped on his arm to stop him. He froze right there with me just hanging in the air from his arm. He looked at me, and I explained that it was a skunk, so he didn't throw the rock. But that picture in my mind of me hanging from his arm—it was the funniest thing you could ever imagine."

The treks to the lake often turned into fishing marathons.

"He could fish for hours and hours, and I was the same way," Crippen said. "We could just sit for hours and talk. We had a system down pat. We knew when the fish were going to bite. They'd bite right at 8 p.m. and then 3 a.m. and then 7 a.m. We would stay out there the whole time. The greatest thing was we really talked and talked about a bunch of stuff. That was probably the time I cherished the most with Kenny. Catching the fish was secondary to the conversation."

Teammate Pat Tyrance also shared the late-night fishing experience with Kenny.

"Kenny loved to fish," Tyrance said. "I went with him because I enjoyed his company more than I enjoyed fishing. There were a couple of occasions where we'd go fishing in the late evening, and he'd fish until early morning. I remember the last time we went, we were at a pond outside of Lincoln. I couldn't go all night, so I went and slept in the car."

Like Crippen, Tyrance said the conversation during those fishing trips—and becoming closer as a friend to Walker—are what he remembers.

"I recall the times we fished, discussing different events concerning the team," Tyrance said. "And since I was what you might call 'challenged' as a fisherman—I wasn't a big fisherman— Kenny would show me the ropes, the dos and don'ts. He was a very funny guy, great sense of humor, lots of fun to be around. If you were close to him, there were no boundaries as to what you could joke about with him. He and Morgan were really tough on each other when it came to joking. And everyone knew that Morgan could get away with saying a lot more to Kenny than anyone else!"

Crippen said Walker was quite the fisherman, but said Kenny did go to extremes.

"Kenny thinks bigger is better," Crippen said. "We'd fish for catfish, which were pretty good sized, but you could catch them with a small pole. The pole Kenny had was unbelievable. It was something you'd catch a marlin with! The pole was as thick around as my wrist, and it was like 15 feet long. The holes where the line went through were the size of Coke cans. He had a big ol' weight on there, way more than he needed. As big and strong as he was, with that huge pole and weight on it, he'd throw that thing darn near across the lake. Heck, when he'd cast and his hook would go in the water, it looked like he already had a fish on it because there was so much weight. Kenny believed you had to have a bigger pole to catch bigger fish. We'd leave the lake, and more often than not, he had the bigger fish. He'd say, 'See, I told you, the bigger pole is better to catch bigger fish.' "

Living off campus with Gregory and Crippen helped prepare Kenny for life. He enjoyed both the freedom and responsibility equally.

"It was a good experience to live off campus," Kenny said. "I had to manage finances for the first time, which was important for me to learn. And we kept the apartment up pretty good in terms of keeping it clean."

A neat freak to this day, Walker was the same way back then.

"When we lived together, he would clean and clean all the time," Crippen said. "He'd get on me and Morgan, 'Clean your room. It's your turn to vacuum. Your turn to do the dishes.' He was always doing the housework. I'm the same way now, but I wasn't then. I'm even particular about my yard—Kenny would be surprised to hear that."

Mimi Mann remembers that side of Kenny, as well.

"He would take it upon himself to help out, and he was just darling," Mann said. "I would be doing something with one of the girls, and Kenny would get it in his head that he was going to clean. I have this table that looks like wood, but it's Formica, and Kenny sprayed it with Pledge to get it to shine. But since it was Formica, the Pledge just left a grease slick on it. I didn't have it in my heart to tell him that he was wrong, so every time he 'cleaned' the table, I'd go back and wipe with a wet rag."

While Mann knows Kenny won't admit it, she believes there is a little bit more of "Tim the Toolman" (from the TV show *Home Improvement*) than Kenny would like to admit.

"We had a really bad lawn mower that you had to pull like 10 to 15 times to start because the throttle never worked," Mann said. "Jim saved and saved and saved and finally got a nice new mower. You'd pull the new mower one time, and that puppy would start right up. Well, Kenny came over, and he was ready to mow the yard for us. He checked the gas and decided he would add a little gas. But he got the chainsaw gas which has oil and gas in it, and would ruin the mower. Jim was yelling as he saw Kenny walking toward the mower with that stuff—forgetting for a moment that all the yelling in the world wouldn't get Kenny's attention. He ran toward Kenny and stopped him at the last second. Kenny was always into fixing things, too. He made a bunch of adjustments on the new mower, nine or 10 of them, and after that, it took us nine pulls to start the thing. But since he was like our own son, we never had the heart to tell him. And since his heart was in the right place, we figured it could go unsaid."

The many sides of Walker fascinated Crippen, who remains in close contact with Kenny to this day.

"That man is a deep guy," Crippen said. "He is as gentle as a teddy bear at times. But if you get on his bad side, he can be tough."

That toughness came out during an evening at the trio's apartment.

"Like any other college roommates, especially football players, there were times when we got on each other's nerves," Crippen said. "I lived with him long enough to know what I could say. But one day, I had some friends over. They were being loud and disruptive, and Kenny complained about it. I went right in front of the television."

"Get out of the way," Kenny said.

Crippen didn't move.

"I'm not taking any crap from you," Crippen said.

"Come on, move," Kenny said.

"Make me," Crippen said. Walker was 6-foot-4, 240. Crippen, a smallish defensive back, was not.

"No problem," Kenny answered sternly, starting to rise to his feet.

"At that point," Crippen said, "I had a series of thoughts race through my mind. I either made the first move, or he would have squashed me. So I charged him. I ran at him and grabbed him around the waist, pushing and driving him all the way into the kitchen. I was feeling pretty proud of myself. Before I took another breath, he had me in a bear hug. He picked me up like I was Raggedy Andy. He had me in the hall and was slamming me into both walls, back and forth. Luckily, I had three football players there. Still, it took them five minutes to get him off of me. That was the scariest moment of my life. Thinking I could take him was the stupidest thing I ever did. But to show you how good of friends we were, the next day we apologized and shook hands."

Crippen claims to have gotten the best of Walker once in practice.

"Ask him about the time I knocked him on his butt," Crippen said with a smile. "That was my greatest moment. Actually, we were on defense coming up to make a tackle, and Kenny was in the wrong position. Of course, he will say I was in the wrong place."

"Jon was in the wrong place," Kenny confirmed.

"Anyway," Crippen said, "I went flying through the hole with my eyes closed, and Kenny didn't know I was coming. I knocked him on his butt. On film the next day, I really gave it to him. Whenever we had a great hit, we always rolled the film back and forth, watching it again and again. Kenny was just dying that day."

"Jon might be sticking to that story," Kenny said with a smile, "but that's not how I remember it."

CHAPTER 7

THE GIRL WHO HAD A DEAF SON

In 1987 Martina Offenburger had an 11-month-old son at home in Omaha as she planned to resume her college education at Creighton. However, unlike Kenny, who was born with hearing and lost it to meningitis, Tommy was born deaf. Martina said doctors believe it was a genetic trait that caused Tommy's deafness.

She met Kenny at a college party in Lincoln during Kenny's sophomore year in Lincoln.

"I was sitting there at a party, talking to Mike Croel," Martina said. "It was a fraternity party, and there were a lot of football players there. My friend and I were talking, and I saw Kenny, who was wearing this golf hat and a pink shirt. My friend said, 'See that guy over there in the pink shirt? He's a football player and he's deaf. I said, 'Oh, that's interesting.' So I went up and introduced myself."

Regardless of his deafness, Martina could sense other traits about Kenny that made him unique.

"I really liked him," Martina said, "and wanted to get to know him. I was just so impressed with the kind of person he was. You see all these athletes who are so bad about how they treat people. Kenny was so nice to me, that even if we didn't have a relationship, I wanted him to be my friend.

"I wasn't serious about him yet," Martina said, "but then I saw him at another party four days later. I thought, 'He won't remember me.' But then he playfully grabbed my hair. I talked to him using sign language."

"I remembered that she was the girl who had a deaf son," Kenny said.

"We talked a lot," Martina said. "He had another deaf friend there at the party. The next day, Kenny played for a Lincoln Association of the Deaf basketball team and invited me to come watch, which I did."

One of Kenny's goals was to let Martina know that whether they became a couple or not, there were a lot of resources she could tap for Tommy.

"I tried to encourage her to look around the deaf community and get to know people," Kenny said.

"He really wanted me to see the deaf community," Martina said.

Kenny started involving Martina and Tommy whenever he did something in the deaf community.

"Kenny took us to a pig roast, and Tommy wanted to see everything," Martina said.

More than two years passed, and Kenny and Martina saw each other only occasionally.

"I saw him about every six months or so, but we had gotten to be good friends," Martina said. "One day he called me out of the blue. I was living in Omaha, and he said, 'Come down to Lincoln.' It was the day before Easter in 1990. So I went down there on a Saturday. I asked him, 'What plans do you have for Easter?' He said, 'Nothing.' I knew my parents would be fine with it.

"We went to my parents' house, and I could tell he was a little concerned," Martina said. "I told him how I grew up going to Catholic school, and, of course, he knew I had a bi-racial son. He could not believe how my family supported my situation and how they embraced him. I could tell by his expression that it was not what he expected. We had a nice time with my family, and then we went to my aunt's house, and he met more of my family.

"It wasn't hard at all to communicate," Martina said. "My parents and everyone in my family could sign a little bit."

"That's not quite right," Kenny said before adding with a smile, "they talked really slow—I had patience."

On a more serious note, Kenny did find the day completely enjoyable and relaxing.

"They made me feel welcome," he said.

Martina's father, Dan Offenburger, had heard of Kenny long before they met.

"I had heard about him from the time Nebraska started recruiting him," Offenburger said. "I knew he was a great athlete and a deaf kid; the question was could he play at that level. I remember thinking, 'That's too bad; he won't get to play much at all.'"

Martina and Kenny were very different, yet her father did not see anything out of the ordinary in their relationship.

"It didn't surprise me when Marti met Kenny because our family had been around a lot of black kids since we lived in Omaha and she went to Central High School, so race was not a factor in how our family picked friends," Offenburger said. "The way Kenny came across to us was as a real nice guy who was real hard for me to understand. But I have been deaf in one ear my whole life, so that made it harder for me to hear him. He seemed like a nice guy."

They dated until the fall of 1990, and then Kenny surprised Martina just before two-a-day football practices started in August.

"See you after the season," Kenny said. "I don't have time for the relationship."

Martina then went through a crisis of her own. A doctor who she says sexually abused both her and her sister was brought up on and later convicted of molesting young female patients. More than 50 women came forward to corroborate what had happened.

"We were talking on the phone through the relay, and somehow Kenny sensed something was wrong and asked why I was upset," Martina said. "I told him what I saw on the news. I told him I could deal with it—I had a sister who died, so I knew how to handle grief. Kenny told me, 'You can't be like that; you have to deal with it and get it out.' I told him that I'd be all right, so a few minutes later we hung up. An hour later, he was at my door in Omaha asking, 'Are you sure you are OK?' I was so surprised that he could talk to me about that."

Kenny's attitude was different. Being deaf, he couldn't imagine that someone with the ability to communicate and hear so easily would want to keep a problem locked inside them.

"Before we started our relationship, I knew she was stubborn," Kenny said. "I forced her to open up, but it took a while."

While the incident had happened when Martina was in junior high, she says she convinced herself to keep it out of her mind. When it got out in the open, she hit an emotional wall.

"I was just so depressed," Martina said. "I was a single mom. I was tired of being broke. And when that happened with the doctor going to jail, it all hit me at once."

Martina was treated for depression but ended up becoming addicted to her medicine. While Kenny didn't have time for the relationship, he made time to see her. And he was stunned.

"When I saw her and what she was going through, she was changing," Kenny said. "She wasn't the same person I had known a month before. It was hard for me. I was trying to become successful and succeed in football."

Martina checked into a treatment center.

"He came to the treatment center, and we talked," Martina said. "We kind of broke it off at that point. I let him go because I had to— I didn't want to. But with everything going on in his life, it wasn't fair that I would bring him down."

Martina's father knew the emotional load Kenny would have to bear to help Martina through the crisis could affect the goals Kenny was setting for his life.

"When I got the call that she was in the hospital in Lincoln, I took a friend of mine, a guy who was in his 90s," Offenburger said. "I went to Kenny's apartment and talked to him. I said, 'Kenny, I appreciate what you have done for her, but you have to take care of your life and your future. You have a right to enjoy it and plan for your future. Marti has to deal with the choices she made. We will be there for her, so you can move on with your life.'

"But he really stuck by her," Offenburger said. "We already liked him a great deal. We just wanted him to know he had no obligation to Marti and Tommy. I knew how hard he had worked. I wanted him to be able to do his best and enjoy it. But he did stick with her, and we appreciated that a lot. They were both learning about their lives at that point. He's a pretty solid human being."

Kenny tried to put Martina out of his mind. But each night he thought about both Martina and Tommy and was worried about both of them.

"I liked Marti right away," Julia Walker said. "They were more friends than anything else, long before they started to date. It was a long courtship. He kind of just fell in love with Tommy and what happened with Kenny and Marti followed."

Less than a week after Martina was hospitalized, Kenny showed up unannounced at the treatment center.

"He showed up out of the blue," Martina said.

"I don't know why I am back," Kenny said, "but I can't stay away."

"I knew she needed some help," Kenny said. "I could not leave her. I had to stay and support her when things weren't going well for her."

Martina said Kenny's sacrifice during that time of her own need was something she will never forget.

"There were times that came up when his pro football career was ending or in a state of transition and I was the strong one for him," Martina said. "But back then, I was the lost person, and he was the strong one."

CHAPTER 8

FINISHING STRONG AT NEBRASKA

A s he grew into his role on the defensive line, Kenny started to fit in better than ever.

"At the time I suggested it," Nebraska defensive coordinator McBride said, "I didn't know if he wanted to play in the defensive line. He was eager for the opportunity. There was a period there where I had to go slow with him, so he wouldn't get discouraged. Once he found he could do it, his work habits were so good, I could see right away that he would be an overachiever. He really thrived on getting better. Kenny has been through so many discouraging things that he knows there will be times when he is challenged. But he took the attitude that he'd just learn from it and be better for the experience."

Walker's workouts in the offseason reached new levels of intensity as he saw the potential reward of being a regular member of the varsity.

"You have to find a way to motivate yourself," Walker said. "You can't let anyone tell you that you can't do it. You have to believe in yourself. You just find another path, another avenue when the one you are trying is blocked."

Pat Tyrance, the starting linebacker, knew Walker was undersized, at 240 pounds, for the defensive line (typical defensive linemen weigh anywhere from 280 to 300 pounds), but like the hearing situation, the size wasn't an issue, either.

"As sophomores we played the same position," Tyrance said. "Our senior year, I actually weighed more than he did. He was strong—obviously he did more than hold his own against the big guys."

Walker, according to McBride, used every tool possible to his advantage.

"For the defensive line, Kenny was a little undersized," McBride said. "But in terms of his size, he had tremendous speed—way more than guys his size ever have. He was also stronger than anyone else his size. So just like he did things to communicate despite being deaf, he compensated for his lack of size on the defensive line with great strength, speed and quickness. Another thing that people don't understand is the importance of hand strength, and Kenny had all kinds of that."

According to then Husker quarterback Gerry Gdowski, Kenny's deafness faded to the background as Walker's play stepped to the forefront.

"I don't think it was really an issue," Gdowski said. "You could understand him quite a bit just having a conversation. I guess as far as that goes, you just had to concentrate a little harder to pick it up. But as you are around him more and more, you learn how he says certain words—just like anyone else, in a lot of ways. I have friends with accents who are hard to understand at first. But the more I am around them, the easier it is to understand them, which is just how it was with Kenny."

Kenny knew his future was bright.

"At that point, the coaches were really happy with me," Walker said. "My quickness and speed were improving more and more. I never really gained that much more weight, but I did get stronger and stronger. It was like I could beat every offensive linemen my senior year. No offensive lineman could stop me."

The continuous praise from the coaches made Walker want to work even more at perfecting his technique. He also kept working hard in the weight room, adding 15 pounds of muscle.

"Even though I was getting better, it was not affecting my work habit at all—by that I mean I wasn't getting complacent by any means," Walker said. "I was working harder, harder and even harder. Life for me, being deaf, was never easy. I could have chosen the easier path and just done my schoolwork. But because of Coach McBride and the fact that I didn't give up, it all started working out."

Tyrance said Walker's work ethic was unsurpassed.

"Like most great athletes, he had a desire to win and to better himself and challenge himself," Tyrance said. "He was a hard worker. It is almost hard to describe how hard he worked. You really had to see it to appreciate it."

On the field any communication problems had been dealt with and were no longer an issue.

"We made sure that when we were calling a play, we looked directly at him," Tyrance said. "He did a great job of reading your lips and interpreting the expression on your face, those kind of things."

McBride set up the film study sessions perfectly. It got to the point where McBride almost forgot Mann was in the room.

"What Charlie had me do was sit at a desk facing Kenny," Mann said. "Kenny was in the front row watching the film, which was on the wall behind me. Charlie sat by Kenny. So Kenny could see the light on my hands, and I could see and hear Coach McBride. So Kenny had me and the film in the same frame of his vision. It was perfect."

McBride was constantly cognizant of possible communication gaps.

"Many people who communicate with deaf people don't realize that you have to be looking at them when you talk if you want them to understand you," McBride said. "If we put in something new, we'd spend time before or after the meeting together to clarify it. It would just be Kenny and I, without anyone else around, except sometimes maybe Mimi."

McBride, who at the time chewed tobacco, kept a cup that he spit in on the desk that Mimi sat behind during film sessions. Mann did not want to be anything more than, as she said, a "telephone." Since a telephone couldn't complain about the cup, she didn't think it was her place to say something, either.

"I wanted to say, 'This is so sick!' The smell just made me nauseous," Mann said. "The fifth year, I decided everyone loves Kenny; he had his own communication strategy, and everything was fine. I figured, 'Good, now I get to be a person, too.' That was the year I told Coach McBride, 'Get this thing out of here!' "

McBride claims he benefited from learning ways to deal with Kenny's situation.

"What Kenny did for me was reinforce the value of communicating—and what a critical component that is to teaching, whether someone can hear or not," McBride said. "I was always aware of Kenny, and I never forgot he was there. When I'd draw things on the blackboard, I'd turn to face the players when I explained it. Or I'd explain before I turned to draw on the board."

Walker never skipped a detail, picking up in preparation what other players might need clarification on during practice.

"Kenny was one of those kids who was probably as thorough as I've ever coached," McBride said. "He was always asking questions—there was always something he wanted to know. He would ask about anything and everything. He was concerned with the details, which as a coach you really like to see."

Being deaf became an asset when McBride saw one of his formations of plays improperly executed.

"There were a lot of little things that Kenny did that were funny," McBride said. "He knew I was upset—although he will say he never did this—and he'd turn away from me so he could not 'hear' me. If I was on the field a ways from him, and he knew I was going to come down on him, he'd turn around. People don't realize what a sharp, witty guy Kenny is unless they get to know him."

Sometimes Kenny would take it one step further. But McBride never bit on it.

"He'd give me a fake-confused look, and I'd say, 'Don't give me this stuff about being deaf; you can hear everything I'm saying,' " McBride recalls with a wide grin.

Tyrance said Kenny and Coach McBride developed their own kind of language.

"Kenny could just look at Coach McBride's face and know what he was saying," Tyrance said. "I don't recall seeing Mimi that often in practices. I remember seeing her in team meetings and things like that, but not as much out there on the field."

At home Kenny worked until the early hours of the morning on homework, determined to be on the dean's list. At practice he worked as hard as anyone, setting a good example for the underclassmen.

"Kenny is a perfectionist, and you see that when you get around him," Crippen said. "He's the hardest working person I have ever been around, physically hard-working and mentally hard-working, studying and learning."

The reason for the hard work was simple.

"I had tried too hard to give up at that point," Kenny said.

Walker had a breakthrough performance his junior year. He did not start, but was a regular. He had 21 total tackles, including seven tackles for a negative 27 yards (five of which were sacks for 24 of those yards). That was the most number of overall tackles for any non-starter on the defense.

An even more impressive statistic was Walker's 12 quarterback "hurries" (forcing the quarterback out of position and making him throw the ball before he was ready), which was second-best on the team. One of those hurries caused an interception at Minnesota. Walker had five tackles against Iowa State, which marked the first of four games in a row in which Kenny had at least one sack.

"The big thing was finding a place for him to play," Osborne said. "We thought he had talent, so it was just a matter of finding a place where he fit in. At linebacker, it was more of a thing of communicating with the secondary calls when guys go in motion. That meant the linebackers' responsibilities changed. Kenny couldn't hear the secondary calls. That was the biggest problem we had there. When he went inside at first on the defensive line, he didn't fit the mold because he wasn't big enough. But he kept getting bigger and stronger. Soon, he was doing very well. He got by on quickness and always being very, very strong. It took a little while for him to grow into that position, but he did it. We played him at linebacker, defensive end, inside on defense, and finally found a place where he could become comfortable. He became a great player."

One of the questions McBride was often asked by out of town media members was how often Walker was penalized for jumping offside or hitting a player late because he could not hear the whistle. McBride said neither was ever an issue. In fact, Walker was among the least penalized players on the defense.

"I remember reading about a deaf kid in New York who filed a lawsuit because the superintendent would not let him play football," McBride said. "They were afraid that the kid, being deaf, would hit kids after the whistle. The irony there is that just the opposite is true; Kenny never had a late hit, and I don't remember him jumping offside, either. His sight was so good that he noticed all the movements when the ball was snapped. And when the play ended, Kenny could tell because of the other players' body language. He didn't need to hear a whistle to know the play was over."

McBride and Walker had developed quite a chemistry.

"The thing with deaf people is they don't get the jokes all the time when they are told," McBride said. "They pick up on the body language and that kind of thing. As Kenny picked that up, we really shared a lot of laughs."

Entering Walker's senior season, greatness was apparent. Walker was Nebraska's fastest lineman and—unbelievably—the sixth fastest player on the whole team with a 4.58-second time in the 40-yard dash. He recorded the third-highest strength index score on the team, bench-pressing 370 pounds.

"Nobody has really blocked Kenny," Coach Osborne said at the time. "He's good, he's strong and he's quick. And we can't seem to slow him down."

No one else slowed Walker, either.

As a senior, Walker started all 11 games at defensive tackle, and had 73 total tackles, second best on the team behind Tyrance. Walker led the team by a wide margin in tackles for losses (21 for 105 yards), sacks (11 for 69 yards) and quarterback hurries (21). At the time the 21 tackles for lost yards and the 11 sacks equaled the second-best single-season totals ever for a Husker. Walker was named the Big Eight's Defensive Player of the Week after the Huskers pounded Oklahoma State, 31-3. But his best game of the season might have come against Oregon State. Walker was all over the place with seven tackles (five for lost yardage), four sacks for 29 yards, two pass breakups and four hurries. Oregon State quarterback Matt Booher had seen enough.

"He can go ahead and play that Big Eight schedule," Booher said at the time, "and I'll just go back to the West Coast."

Walker posted nine tackles twice, against Kansas and K-State.

His list of honors came from both the classroom and the field. He posted a 3.1 grade point average as a junior to earn Academic All-Big Eight honors.

On the field, Walker was selected first-team All-American by the Associated Press, the Football Writers, *The Sporting News* and the *Football News*. He was a semifinalist for the Outland Trophy, given each year to the nation's top lineman. He repeated as a first-team All-Big Eight pick and earned nearly a dozen other honors, including a pair of Player of the Week awards. While Osborne was the one who gave Walker the opportunity to go to Nebraska, it was Charlie McBride who saved Walker from leaving during his days as a lost, position-less soul. So it was only appropriate that McBride gave Walker the news.

"I went into my office, and I could see Kenny was already in there," McBride said. "It was going through my mind, gosh, about all the hard work that kid did. He stood when I entered the room, and I told him he made All-American, and he hugged me. We sat down, and we both cried like a couple of babies. There was just so much that went into that for that young man. To fathom what he accomplished against such great odds just made me so proud of him."

Nebraska assistant coach Ron Brown said it is important that people realize that it took a lot more than just being a great football player for Walker to make All-American.

"There were times when I had to talk to him, and I understood him very clearly," Brown said. "It wasn't without its difficulties. But once he found his spot, the transition went very well. To become a first-team All-American is impressive, but to understand he had to fit into context of what we were doing makes it that much more impressive. You don't become an All-American just running around on the football field. You have to take care of your responsibilities on every play and put the team first. That's what Kenny did."

McBride is the kind of coach who is loved by all his players. Truth be told, if McBride ever needed a kidney, the hospital would have to hire security because the line would be wound around the block with former players looking to help the man whom they hold in such high regard.

Mann said few outside the program have seen the soft side of McBride. So while Mann is grateful to Kenny for the credit he gives her for his success, Mann said McBride was the one who made it all work out.

"My role was to translate the message from the coach to Kenny," Mann said. "I have to credit Charlie McBride—I just adore that man. Charlie tries to give a gruff image, but he is the softest, sweetest man I have ever known. He is just a teddy bear. The man I have seen is so different from the one portrayed on TV and in the newspaper. I remember he was recruiting someone and he got a call one day telling him that the kid had a brain tumor. I walked into his office as he hung up the phone, and he told me about it. He just started crying, and he wasn't embarrassed about that at all. He told me all about the kid, how special he was and how much Coach wanted to work with him and help him get a college education."

McBride went to any imaginable extent to make things work for Walker, trying new things to ensure Walker had every chance to succeed.

"Charlie did anything it took to make it work." Mann said. "No amount of time was too much for Charlie to say it again, to say it in a different way, to review the information or to quiz Kenny. The mental part sunk through to Kenny because of the persistence of Coach McBride. And Charlie got a player who was one of the best in the country his junior and senior seasons."

Tyrance, an Academic All-American and All-Big Eight pick, said Walker was especially smart to build on his strengths, which, Tyrance believed, made Walker's deafness a moot point.

"Obviously, he was a great athlete, very strong and quick," Tyrance said. "I think more than anything, he probably compensated for his hearing deficit by having very keen eyesight. I remember times when Kenny would jump because he saw an offensive lineman move, drawing a penalty on the offense. Yet, none of the rest of us saw the movement. Kenny was just so in tune with his vision that he detected things the rest of us didn't always see. Sure, he was a very good athlete and very strong, and had good speed. But I think it was his eyesight that more than compensated for his deafness."

McBride said Walker's hard work, coupled with a lot of talent, made him the ideal player.

"Kenny was a guy who, first of all, was really instinctive," McBride said. "To be such a very instinctive football player is, in some ways, a God-given thing. Of course, Kenny is more visually aware of things going on around him because he doesn't hear. So while he can't hear, he's actually more alert to some things than other players are. He had no obstructions from the outside noises, so playing a road game in a loud stadium never affected him."

Gerry Gdowski, the Huskers' quarterback at the time, said Walker could have played college basketball as well, had he so chosen.

"Kenny is just an unbelievable athlete," Gdowksi said. "Morgan Gregory and I played on an intramural basketball team with Kenny. He could do anything he wanted on the basketball court, too. He was just a great athlete."

The Huskers switched defenses over the years, going with players about Walker's size at the defensive end position, which was changed to "rush end" because those players are expected to pressure opposing quarterbacks. While Walker was a bit undersized for a defensive tackle, he would be the prototype today for a rush end.

"He had great speed," Gdowski said. "If you go just as far as athleticism, he's among the best that have ever been at Nebraska. He was very strong. It was just a matter of him fitting into the right system on defense. I believe toward the end of his career at Nebraska, the coaches went to the 4-3 style, especially in passing situations. That's where Kenny excelled—as a pass rusher. If he played in the defense now at Nebraska where he was a rush end, you'd be talking about Kenny being as good as Trev Alberts or Grant Wistrom because athletically Kenny was up there with those guys, the best to ever play the position at Nebraska."

CHAPTER 9

A BROTHER'S LOVE

The sounds of war echoed through the night as Warrant Officer Gus Walker curled up in his tent in January of 1991, during the war in the Persian Gulf. A helicopter pilot, Walker was with his U.S. Army unit in the desert of Saudi Arabia.

The next day's sun would bring another list of supplies and troops for Gus to ferry wherever it was needed. But on this night, as the wind whipped the sand against his tent, Walker had his radio tuned to the Armed Forces Network because Gus' "little" brother Kenny—always referred to as "Ken" by Gus—was playing in the Japan Bowl, a college all-star game. Kenny had just finished his brilliant football career at Nebraska and was giving pro scouts and coaches a preview of what they could expect if they could overlook his deafness and draft him.

Every time Gus heard Kenny's name called during the game, he screamed and cheered as though he was a fan in Tokyo, not a warrior in the Gulf War.

"It was 2 a.m., so I know I probably woke up the guys in the tents around me," Gus says with a smile. "Heck, I bet the Iraqis could have heard me the way I was yelling."

As the game progressed, the radio announcer said he was going to cut to a radio interview with one of the players. That player was Kenny Walker. As an interpreter translated Kenny's words, Gus could understand his brother's voice perfectly well in the background.

"I am thinking about my brother Gus," Kenny said. "He is in the Persian Gulf. I know he is listening tonight—he listens to anything that has Nebraska football in it! I am proud of my brother, and I want him to know that I am worried about him."

Gus thrust a fist in the air.

"I was going crazy," Gus said.

The ecstasy turned to a more tangible emotion, that of the love of a brother. Gus started to cry as he heard his brother talk about him.

"I couldn't believe it," Gus said. "Here Ken was at an all-star game, and all he wants to do is talk about how he is proud of me. That was his moment, and for him to dedicate it to me like that really says a lot about who Ken is."

It also speaks volumes about the relationship between Kenny and Gus, two years Kenny's senior. As the second youngest of the Walker's six children, Gus was the one who was with Kenny in the beginning, middle, and all the way up through Kenny's sophomore year in high school.

Gus knew first and foremost that Kenny was his little brother. At first because Gus was just a child and knew nothing different, Kenny's deafness was never an issue. As Gus entered his elementary school years, he realized Kenny was different, but Gus was determined to make sure Kenny never thought of himself as different.

"As a kid, you don't realize that (the deafness) as being something special," Gus said. "Ken was my brother—that's all I knew. That's how things were, so that's just how it was. No one felt sympathy for him. I was the older brother, so I expected him to do things at my level. When I did things with my friends, Kenny would play with us, so he had to play at that level. He had to be just as good as us. I didn't take his hearing disability or his age into it. He had to do things just like we did in order to play with us. When you grow up in a neighborhood, you have to be able to perform at whatever level the kids you are playing with are. None of us cared if Kenny could hear as long as he could catch, run and throw. I was tough on him. I never accepted any excuses."

Kenny did not have to fight a lot because of his deafness, Gus chose to address the conflicts himself.

"Back then, people—kids especially—weren't that educated about deaf people," Gus said. "People would say, 'Deaf and dumb,' and the two words could not be separated. I would tell kids who said that, 'Rephrase what you just said, or you will get punched.' I wouldn't tell Ken what was going on because I didn't want him to know. I viewed it as this: the things about which he was not aware would not affect his self-esteem. I'd be fighting, and Ken would just be screaming to know why I was fighting. I wouldn't pass along that information to him. I never wanted to hear Ken say, 'I am different from everyone else.' My goal was to never make him believe he was different. It was hard for me to deal with it as his brother, so I would know how much harder it would have been for him to deal with it personally."

Kenny did not back down from the challenges, and—like any little brother—would question his older brother's authority whenever he disagreed with Gus.

"We fought all the time—it was like a daily ritual," Gus said. "We'd go out and my mom would say, 'If you are going out, Gus, take your little brother.' So I'd say, 'Yes, ma'am,' and off we'd go. I'd tell Kenny, 'If you're going with me, you do things my way.' Being kids, if he didn't like something, we'd get into it. We didn't throw punches or anything, but we'd fight like any other brothers."

They would fight with a passion that was matched only by the one apparent when they felt like they'd hurt each other's feelings.

"One trip in particular stands out," Gus said. "Ken and I were going to Oklahoma with my brother-in-law. We were fighting over who would sit in the front seat. We were junior-high age. It was early in the morning, and it was like there was no way either one of us was going to give in. After a while we felt so bad about how we were fighting that we both suggested that the other one sit in the front seat. And that almost turned into a fight, because he wanted me to sit in the front since he felt badly about what he said, and I wanted him to sit in the front because I felt badly about what I said. It was one of those times that, when I look back, showed how much we really loved each other."

Kenny was competitive with Gus in just about everything.

"He was quite the fisherman, even back then," Gus said. "My mother would take us fishing every Saturday. If we didn't have money for bait, that was no problem for Ken. He'd mix dough or corn and use that for bait—and it would work every time! The one thing he did that drove me crazy was that whenever someone would catch a fish, before they could even reel it in, Ken was right there casting his line in because that's where the fish were. He was so bad about that, that he'd tangle up his line in yours, the whole works. He was quite the aggressive fisherman."

Gus also used every big-brother trick he could think of on Kenny.

"I'd take a candy bar, and since we were of limited means, we would usually only get one, so we'd have to share it," Gus said. "I'd never break it evenly. I'd go maybe 60-40—on purpose, of course. I'd say, 'Wait Ken, this isn't even. Let me even it up so it's fair.' So I'd eat the 60 half until it was down to where it was even with the smaller half. Then I'd say, 'There you go, now it's even.' He'd buy it every time. I always wondered when he'd catch on. But that had nothing to do with him being deaf. It's just something that older brothers do to younger brothers."

When the family lived in Denver, Kenny caught a special bus to school with other kids who had disabilities, so he had to leave almost an hour before Gus did each morning.

"He was always waiting until the last minute on things," Gus said. "We had to share a room almost the whole time growing up— it was like Felix and Oscar. I was so neat, and he was so messy that we had put a line of tape down the middle of the room one time to section our sides off. I'd lay my clothes out ahead of time, the whole works. Well, one morning he's flying around the room, and he ends up with my clothes on. He was a couple of inches taller than me, so he comes home that day in pants that didn't even reach his ankles."

"There was another time when I got sick of his last-minute routine when he was in sixth grade," Gus said, "so I set the clocks ahead an hour. He was crashed the next morning, and I woke him up. 'Ken, Ken! You're late!' Ken looked at the clock, 'Oh no!' He ran around and got ready. He was standing at the door, 'Oh no, I missed my bus!' I told him what I had done, and he was mad! But he had plenty of time to burn that morning."

His mother did not allow Kenny any leeway, either.

"When we were living in Denver, Ken had picked up some bad language—some curse words," Gus said. "We were in our room arguing, and his back was to our door. I could hear my mom coming, so I stopped, and Ken kept on going, just cursing me out.

Kenny and his brother Augusta (Gus).

Kenny in first grade with his first hearing aid. (left)

Kenny in third grade. (below)

Kenny became a standout player during junior high as he grew to love sports.

Kenny's high school years kept him actively involved in many sports, including basketball and track.

Kenny (57) in the
Nebraska defensive
huddle during the
1990 season.

Kenny makes one
of his many tackles
during his senior
season. (left)

Senior Day, 1990. Kenny's last
home game at Nebraska. Kenny
is stunned to see 76,000 fans
giving him "the deaf applause."

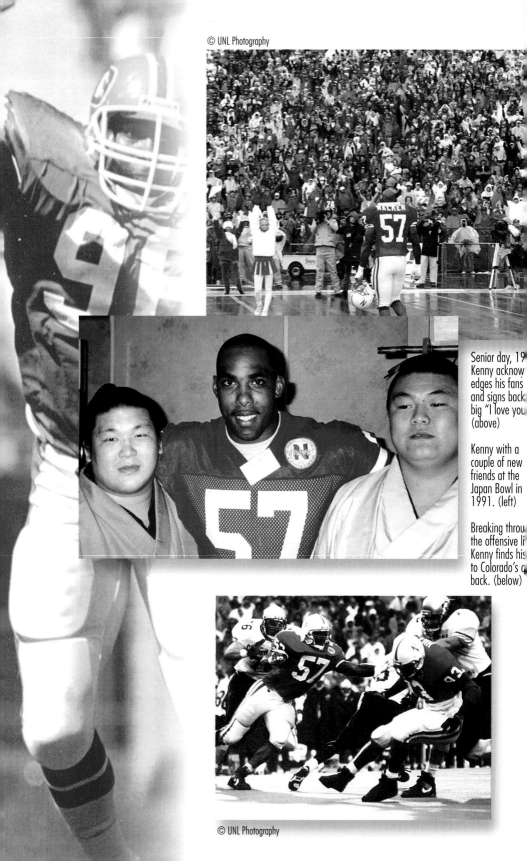

Senior day, 19
Kenny acknow
edges his fans
and signs back
big "I love you
(above)

Kenny with a
couple of new
friends at the
Japan Bowl in
1991. (left)

Breaking throu
the offensive li
Kenny finds his
to Colorado's q
back. (below)

ALL ROOKIE TEAM

Kenny Walker   DE

Number 96 for the Denver Broncos,
1991-1993.

Kenny's Bronco rookie card. (right)

Kenny with interpreter Mimi Mann on the Bronco field.

February 14, 1992, Dan and Mary Jean Offenburger (left), mother Julia and brother Gus Walker (right) help Kenny and Martina celebrate their wedding day.

Kenny with a student at a Steamboat Springs, CO, elementary school in 1992. (right)

Kenny and Martina with an NFL referee and his wife during an NFL cruise, February, 1992. (below)

WELCOME KENNY WALKER

A deaf class in Steamboat Springs, CO, welcomes Kenny during the spring of 1992. (top)

Kenny with his latest catch in the pan! (left)

Kenny with his parents Fred and Julia Walker. (below)

Bo sportin' his new Nebraska Cornhusker bib, 1993.

Kenny and the boys in another wrestling match, 1996.

While visiting his brother Darron's family, Kenny hugs Tommy (age 6), Bo (7 months) and Aleena Walker (5 months).

The boys showing off their muscles (and their car)!

A 1994 horseback ride in the Canadian Rockies at a friend's horse ranch.

Kenny and Bo square off while wearing their Calgary helmets.

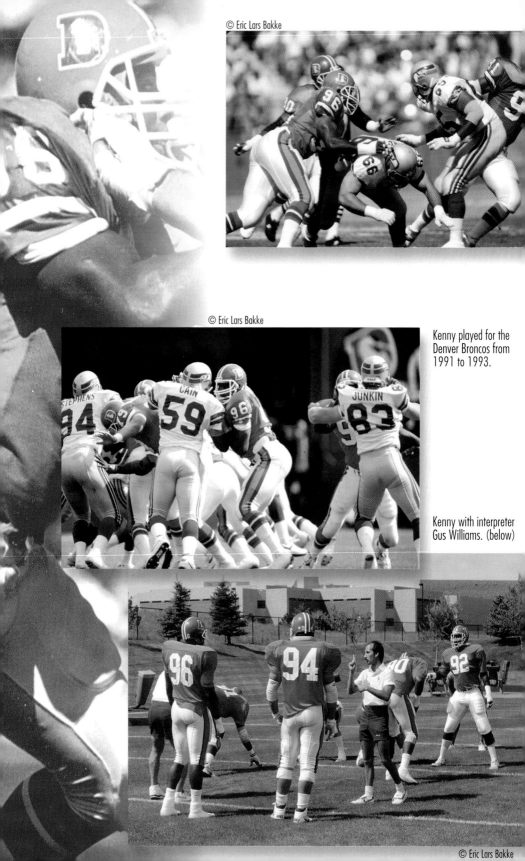

Kenny played for the
Denver Broncos from
1991 to 1993.

Kenny with interpreter
Gus Williams. (below)

Kenny and his dad. (above)

Kenny challenges Bo to a race car video game. (left)

Another Kenny Walker football card. (below)

KENNY WALKER DE
PACIFIC

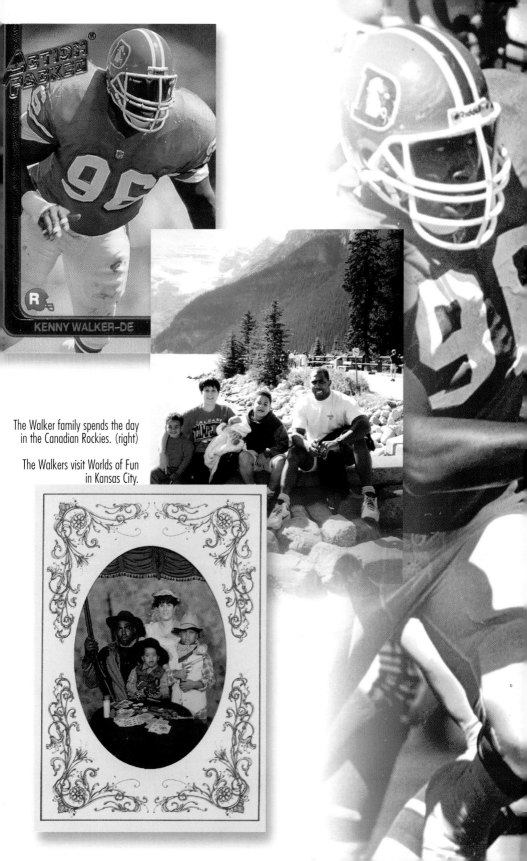

KENNY WALKER-DE

The Walker family spends the day in the Canadian Rockies. (right)

The Walkers visit Worlds of Fun in Kansas City.

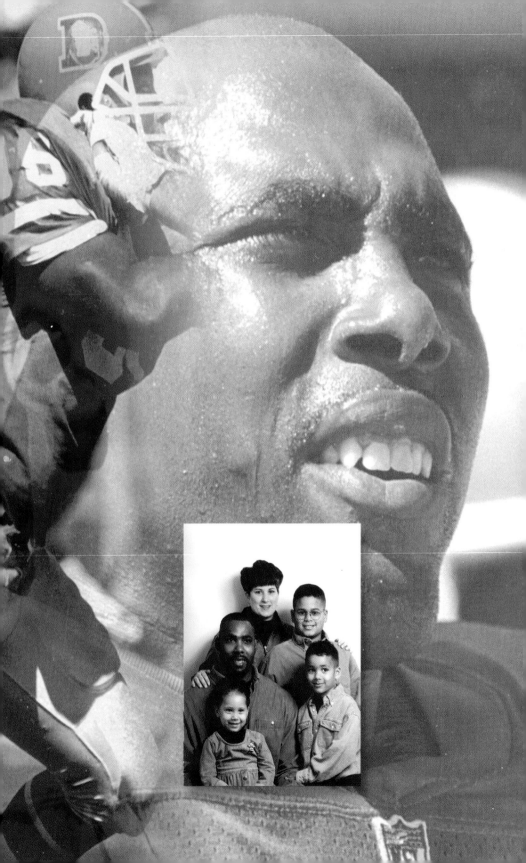

My mom stood there in the doorway and listened for a minute, and then tapped him on the shoulder. He turned and faced her. The first words out of his mouth were, 'Gus started it.' Now that was funny."

Living in Denver, the family had a dog—Yogi—a little terrier Kenny was very fond of.

"That was really the only dog we ever owned," Gus said. "Ken was maybe five years old when we got that dog. Ken could not say 'Yogi'—Ken called it 'Gowee,' and that dog came running to him every time. The rest of us would call it 'Gowee,' and it wouldn't come. That dog just loved Ken. I remember when we moved back to Crane, we had to get rid of Yogi. That was hard on Ken. He really loved that dog."

Gus remembers scores of examples of Kenny's sensitive side.

"This just shows you the type of person he is," Gus said. "We only had one bicycle most of the time. But Ken got one for Christmas when he was starting junior high. We went to City Park in Denver and went out on the paddle boats. My bike was stolen. Ken insisted on giving me his bicycle. I kept telling him no, that this bike was his. He made me take his. I think about that now—I can't even imagine my own kids sharing their little toys, much less a bicycle. That was the only bicycle he had. Ken's love was so unconditional and knew no limits. That is what, to me, makes Ken so special."

Gus said Kenny was among the best track athletes ever at Crane High School.

"I was a senior when Ken was a sophomore," Gus said. "I was a good long jumper. In our first meet, Ken had to jump against me. I remember this vividly because he jumped great, 21 feet—but he jumped off the wrong foot! And he still went 21 feet. He was just a super athlete. He won the sectional high jump as a sophomore. He won so many medals that year that it was hard to keep track of them. Literally, he won almost everything he entered. We'd all wear our medals around, showing them off. But not Ken. He'd put his medals in a box—that is what he did with every one of them. And then he'd give them away to someone who he thought would really enjoy them—he gave a bunch of them to one of my nephews. That tells what sports meant to Kenny; he was in it just for the spirit of competition and to do his best. That's what sports is in its purist form—how Kenny approached it and what he accomplished. He did it for fun and to win. His attitude was, 'I will do my best, and by doing that, I will have fun.' "

Kenny competed with a vengeance, but Gus and the other boys on Crane's basketball, football and track teams wanted to see more fire from Kenny.

"He competed extremely hard," Gus said. "He'd kill the competition and then want to make friends with them. We'd try to motivate him by getting him mad, but it wasn't easy to do that with Ken. I'd say, 'Ken, that guy on the other team wants to hurt you on this play.' Ken would say, 'Why? He doesn't even know me. Why would he try to hurt me?' I'd be like, 'Ken, this guy says you aren't very good.' Ken would say, 'What would make him say something like that? I am pretty good, and I try very hard.' He was too smart and too sensitive to motivate in those macho ways."

Kenny's motivation came from a desire to succeed.

"He didn't score a point in our first game when he was a sophomore on our basketball team," Gus said. "He was our center, and he could jump higher than anyone, and he was stronger than anyone. Not scoring really motivated him. He came out the next game, hit jump shots and slam dunks, and scored 40 points. He felt like he had failed, and maybe there were some people who thought he couldn't really play basketball. So he set out to prove everyone wrong. Whenever someone told him he couldn't do something, I guarantee you Ken came back and did it. There was no challenge that was too big."

Kenny's basketball career actually started three years earlier when Kenny was in the seventh grade.

"Everyone in our neighborhood played basketball, and Kenny was the worst when he first started playing," Gus said. "I was on an eighth grade team, and Kenny was on the seventh grade team at our community center. We beat him bad, and I scored a lot of points against his team even though I played only two quarters. I knew he couldn't play—he couldn't shoot a jumper. He'd use two hands and shoot the ball over the backboard. His team was so bad it came in last place that year and didn't win a game. That really hurt him. He worked on shooting and everything and turned out to be not just a good player the next year, but a great player. The next year Ken's team came in first place. They went from last to first in one year. The kids who were the best ones in the league were afraid to play against Ken. He could jump up and block their shots. They'd drive the lane and put up the shot—then they'd see the ball back around halfcourt after Ken swatted it away. That right there—losing all of his games the first year—was the perfect opportunity for him to say, 'I can't stand this. I will do something else.' So he worked and worked his tail off, and the next year—and in the years to follow—he was always the best player in the league."

One of Kenny's challenges came early on the football field. Playing with kids in the neighborhood, Kenny was playing rough— against bigger kids, nonetheless.

"We tried to teach him to tackle the correct way—you know, to wrap up the guy he was tackling around the waist," Gus said. "But Ken would just clothesline the guy with the ball. He'd just stick his arm out, and that would catch the guy on the Adam's apple, and the guy would go down hard. We were like, 'Ken, you have to stop doing that.' In our family and neighborhood, the big thing was to be a basketball player. But from day one, Ken would say, 'I will be a football player when I get older.' "

As Kenny's interest in football grew entering high school, so did Kenny—physically.

"He was starting to develop, and he did weird things to get stronger," Gus said. "He'd pick up dumpsters and put them on their side and then stand them back up. He kept doing it until he could do it with one arm. I'd say, 'Ken, leave those things alone!' I look back now, and I realize how that was just part of his quest to become all he could be. And becoming that meant getting stronger. Since we couldn't join a gym and didn't have weights, Ken would just lift whatever he could get his hands on."

The most important challenge for Kenny was school.

"I worried about him in high school," Gus said. "The older I got, the more important I realized it was that Ken got an education. He really needed that, more so than anyone else in our family. I knew that to get through life, Ken needed a college education. It was important that he become as educated as he could be."

The learning process was trying for Kenny. But Gus made sure there were no shortcuts.

"When we did homework together, he'd ask me questions just trying to get the answer out of me—which was normal because I know I did that to my older brothers and sisters," Gus said. "I said, 'Ken, you meet the challenge. Look up the word, get the definition and sound it out.' He learned a lot of things in the process of looking words up. He'd say words, and I'd correct him. I was critical of his speech. But he got a lot of confidence using the dictionary, and he used that to his advantage."

Gus worries now that he was perhaps too hard on Kenny.

"It's ironic because as an adult, I look back and feel guilty because I was that way with Ken," Gus said. "I think maybe I should have been more compassionate and understanding. But maybe it was best that I treated him like I did everyone else. Ken really looked up to me, and I realized that. Everything I told him, he took as gospel. It made me mature a lot. I couldn't make things up—it was very important that I got things straight."

Part of Ken's educational quest involved moving the family to Denver from Crane for elementary school through junior high and then back to Crane for high school.

"As I look back, we all made sacrifices," Gus said. "It was hard on all of us. My mother had to deal with financial and personal troubles, and we all went through various things. But Ken made the biggest sacrifice when we moved back to Crane. Here he was in Denver in an environment he was totally comfortable with, and he had to go to a new environment. I knew it would be difficult for him. At Crane, Ken had to focus on the teacher and reading lips because he didn't have the interpreter for every class like he did in Denver."

As coach Rickey White said, Gus was there for Kenny during Kenny's first year at Crane High School.

"After his first year at Crane High School, I realized he was going to be just fine because everyone loved Ken for his personality," Gus said. "But Ken still had to persevere. For anyone else, Ken's move to Crane from Denver was like you or me going to a foreign school where you don't speak their language. That is something very difficult, but Ken managed to do it. The teachers at Crane were very supportive, but they didn't cut him any slack, just as it had to be."

When Kenny was going through his struggles during his sophomore year at Nebraska, he took a long bus ride to Fort Knox in Kentucky where Gus was stationed.

"So many things were going on in his life," Gus said. "There was school, fitting in, football and other things in his personal life. Ken said, 'Gus, I'm thinking about not going back. Football is not fun.' I said, 'Ken, you have to perform or you will lose your scholarship.' So we changed his priorities. We just completely changed them. The only goal was this: graduation. It was like, 'Ken, where are you now, at this point?' He wasn't on the honor roll. We came up with what he needed to accomplish to graduate. I told him, 'Stop looking down the road at the long-term. Just look at your next step. Let's see where you want to go and backtrack to where you are now. What step do you take from here? Where do you want to be?' Kenny said, 'OK, this is what I want to do,' and he talked about how he needed to get his degree, and so on. So we talked about football being a tool to help him build toward his goal. I wanted him to enjoy football, not to look at it as a stress situation. He was putting so much pressure on himself to be the best. Football was important, but not that important. So we talked about football as being the way to pay for education. If he made the NFL, that would just be icing on the cake—but the goal was not to be an NFL player; the goal was to graduate. It all came back to graduating. So we decided to have fun, find what Kenny is good at, use his God-given talents and just be the best he can be. But none of that would happen if he didn't concentrate on his grades. Everything else was a steppingstone to his graduation. The last day, Ken looked at me and said, 'I will go back and have fun, and make schoolwork my priority.' "

Kenny did just that. Soon thereafter, everything fell into place on the football field as well.

"The first year he went back, it was just amazing," Gus said. "He was a different player and a different student. He was doing great things. His grades came up. The picture became clearer for him. He was all right. He just needed a little guidance. He went back and had a great junior year, an even better senior year, and got drafted into the NFL."

As Kenny was preparing for the Broncos' training camp, he went back to see Gus at Fort Knox.

"He was fishing all the time when he wasn't working out," Gus said. "I'd either drop him off at the lake or the gym each morning and then come back and get him in the early evening when I'd get off work. He worked out so hard, it was just incredible. There's this place called Agony and Misery Hill—they are two hills that go almost straight up in the air. Ken would run them as hard as he could. Then, when I'd pick him up, I'd put the parking brake on in my car, and he'd push it a couple of hundred yards. But he was eating and eating and eating, so he put on a lot of muscle, probably 20 pounds. I called my mom and said, 'Mom, send food money. Ken's eaten up all my groceries!' In the evenings, we'd sit at home and go through his playbook. I put together flash cards and computer printouts. Ken knew all the formations and sets. The coaches were amazed at how he knew the whole playbook inside and out when he got to Denver."

Gus remembers Kenny always wanting others to have what they needed before he met his own needs.

"When he became a father—when Krishna was born—when he was still at the University of Nebraska, he was already pretty broke," Gus said. "He'd take all the money he could get and send it to her, to try and be as responsible as he could be under the circumstances. He came to see me one time when he was a sophomore at Nebraska, and he had no jacket. I said, 'Ken, where's your jacket? This is your second winter at Nebraska. Where's your coat?' He said, 'I don't have a jacket. But that is all right because I am strong, and I can make it without one.' I had to beg him to take an old jacket of mine. That same visit, he was wearing these old, ratty shoes. When I went to see him a few years later when he was with the Broncos, those shoes crossed my mind for some reason while I was traveling to Denver. I thought, 'No way he has those same shoes.' He opens the door at his house, and there he is in the shoes, and they look even worse than I'd remembered. But that's Kenny; he'd rather use the money on other people than himself because he enjoys that more."

Although he can point to hundreds of examples of Kenny's compassion for others, Gus is most thankful to have Kenny as a brother.

"I can't say enough about how much he means to me," Gus said.

"Ken is just a gift from God. His life was given to us so others can learn from him."

CHAPTER 10

MORE HONORS OFF THE FIELD

Kenny Walker gained Academic All-Conference honors for his standout 3.10 grade-point average as an art major. Art was a big part of Walker's life from the time he was four years old. Especially as he had to learn to speak again, the art helped Kenny communicate his thoughts, not just to other people, but to himself— it helped him understand his own feelings.

"I speak and express my thoughts through art—pictures have so much language in them," Walker said. "As a child, it helped me relax and express myself about what I could see though my eyes. I would do art at night when I was a child and couldn't sleep. I did this instead of reading books."

In addition to giving Kenny a way to express himself, he loved the dichotomy of art—that it is, at once, simple and complex.

"Art is pure and simple," Kenny said. "It just fascinated me."

Although most people recognize Walker for his exploits on the football field and as a member of the deaf community, art has also influenced his life greatly.

"The reality of art lives in me," Walker said. "It is a part of me."

Walker also likes the sense of ownership he feels in his art.

"It's like it's mine, and I put my emotions in the picture," Walker said. "There are so many ways in art to put emotion in your drawings, paintings or sculptures."

Professor Pat Rowan, one of Kenny's art teachers at the University of Nebraska, said Walker's persistence in the classroom was no less impressive than his persistence on the football field.

"The one thing that Kenny had going for him was he worked hard," Rowan said. "In my 30 years here at Nebraska, I have dealt with lots of student-athletes. Kenny would not give up. He was very responsible and diligent, and a majority of student-athletes are not that way. Art—and all of his studies—were very important to him."

Once the communication barriers were hurdled and other gaps were bridged, Walker was just like any other student.

"Initially, it was extremely difficult for him to come here," Rowan said. "To communicate with various studio art teachers, trying to explain things to them and vice versa was difficult at first for everyone involved. But Kenny persevered."

On top of that Walker was very important to his teachers and classmates.

"All the instructors he had and the students in his classes just loved him," Rowan said. "People in his classes were in awe of him. He was always eager to participate verbally in class critiques. Whether on his own or with Mimi, he had extremely constructive and insightful things to say about his work and others' work. He was a valuable part of the program while he was here."

Walker confirms that the classroom discussions were among his favorite times at Nebraska.

"I love to learn about how someone makes his/her art," Walker said. "I love to listen to artists talking about their art. Some people might find it boring, but not me. And even when someone was talking on and on about something, and other students were getting bored, I wasn't. Those were some of the most interesting parts to me because art is such a big part of who I am."

How good is Walker's art? Good enough to be stolen. It happened during Walker's final semester before graduating at Nebraska.

"I had two oil paintings that I put in this area where we always put our paintings to dry," Walker said. "I came back, and they were gone. I was pretty mad about that. Now, I just hope whoever has them really enjoys them."

While Walker claims to be grateful for everything he learned from Rowan, the professor feels the same way about his former pupil.

"He confirmed my own belief that if someone really wants something badly enough, they can get whatever they want," Rowan said. "He's just a good example of someone like that."

Rowan knew firsthand of Kenny's involvement in the community.

"My son is an athlete, and he was strongly influenced by Kenny. Kenny used to go to all the elementary schools and speak to the kids about staying in school, staying off drugs and trying their hardest. Kenny's sphere of influence was much greater than just the football field. He would talk about staying away from drugs and alcohol and believing in God. He was a real messenger for kids in the elementary schools. I had two kids in elementary school at the time. In one way or another, most of the kids who heard Kenny speak were positively influenced by him."

Rowan has seen thousands of art majors during his three-decade tenure at Nebraska. However, he said Walker's talent was so substantial that everyone noticed his work.

"He has a certain amount of ability, some of it is an inherent ability, and he also has a high degree of facility for making art," Rowan said. "He has a certain innate direction and focus for making art."

Rowan said Walker's talents extended beyond painting into sculptures and drawing.

"I believe he could make a living as an artist," Rowan said. "The art market today is very strange and fickle. Someone with his talent and abilities and reputation would be very marketable."

Rowan's respect for Kenny is matched only by Walker's respect for his former professor.

"Professor Rowan was a very good teacher," Kenny said. "He really motivated me. I saw him every day through the years I was in Lincoln."

Kenny's high school coach at Crane remembers the artistic talent Kenny displayed.

"Kenny was quite the fisherman, so when I told him I was going fishing, he decided to have some fun with it," White said. "Kenny is an artist—I mean a really, really good one. He drew this picture of me holding this fish proudly in a boat—only the boat had a big hole in it, and I was taking on water. He made a joke and made me laugh with that picture. Whether he was deaf or could hear, he'd have been a very, very special person."

CHAPTER 11

A DAY TO REMEMBER

On November 3, 1990, Kenny Walker played his last game at the University of Nebraska's Memorial Stadium.

Unknown to Walker and Mimi Mann before the game, the Big Red's fans were looking for a proper sendoff for Walker. The fans had opened their arms to Walker just as he opened their world to his silent world.

Signs adorned the stadium. One said, "We love you, Kenny," and another said, "Thank you, Kenny and Mimi."

Knowing Kenny could not hear the applause, the area newspapers spent the previous week educating fans on how to "applaud" for a deaf person, waving their hands in the air. So 76,000 fans, many holding red or white handkerchiefs, waved their love for Kenny Walker as he was introduced for the final time as a Husker.

It wasn't the best weather conditions, as a cold rain pelted Walker and the fans. The Huskers also fell short during the game, losing to rival Colorado. But what happened between Walker and the fans that day will be remembered far longer than the outcome of the game.

During home games in Lincoln for the 1997 season, the HuskerVision scoreboard TV screen showed a clip of Walker on the field that day. For Walker, the memory is as clear as day.

Standing just outside the tunnel from where the Huskers enter the field, Walker was, along with all the other seniors, introduced individually before the game. Coach Tom Osborne gave each player a handshake. For Walker, that small display would not be enough. He hugged Osborne before heading on the field, grateful for the opportunity and resources the legendary coach provided for him during Walker's five years in Lincoln.

"I went out on the field, and Coach Osborne shook my hand and said, 'Good luck. Congratulations.' I hugged him, and I cried," Walker said. "Actually, I had cried on the bus on the way over to the stadium. My whole body was numb. It's difficult to put it in words. I wasn't looking forward to that last home game. That was so special to me. I was amazed that people could care that much about me. All the hard work that I put in, I should have been happy about it because everything had paid off. I gave everything I had to Nebraska, and the coaches, the school, the teachers, and the fans gave me everything they had, too. That was just too much for me. The emotion was running through my veins from head to toe. There was just something inside of me that day as I realized that was going to be my last time at Memorial Stadium with Coach Osborne and all the Nebraska people and my teammates. It had been a trying five years, but it had been a great five years, the best years of my life to that point."

Mann was overwhelmed. Kenny's mother, Julia, was in town for the game.

"When the fans all signed, 'I love you' and gave him the deaf applause," Mann said, "for me, that was emotional overload—it was just too much to take it all in. Julia was freezing cold; I was worried about her. I took her into the pressbox because she was freezing, and I was usually in the pressbox on game day so the coaches would know where to find me if they needed me—I wasn't on the sidelines for most games."

In addition to the moisture coming from the cold skies, there was plenty of moisture coming from warm hearts.

"Julia and I were sentimental, so we both cried," Mann said. "I was thinking about what had happened on the field, and that was so touching in itself. But then, the secretaries had all gone in together and gotten a red corsage for me to wear, and Julia had on an almost identical one. All of these things going on, me losing Kenny, Julia losing Kenny, and me losing Julia, were just too much to take in one day. It was a horribly cold, dark biting day, and we were playing this creepy team that treated our fans horribly."

Julia said she finally got a grasp—just that day—of what Nebraska meant to Kenny, and vice versa.

"I really, really cried that day," Julia said. "I remember something else; the next day one of the newspapers said I didn't cry, which was the furthest thing from the truth. My girlfriend next to me at the game could tell you how hard I cried because it was very emotional and heartwarming. It made me feel so good."

The emotion affected men as equally as it did women.

"When that happened, I cried," McBride said. "That was just unbelievable. It is so hard because you know each year that there are seniors who you will lose after the season ends. Losing Kenny was a tough thing to go through because we were pretty close by then."

Osborne, known for his intense focus before games, took a moment to gaze around the stadium at the 150,000-plus hands waving in the air.

"I remember when he went out on the field and everyone was waving their handkerchiefs," Osborne said. "That was a really nice gesture. I remember that moment. That was a very nice time for Kenny; it showed how much fans cared about him."

Coach Ron Brown remembers that moment because it showed the power of the human spirit.

"Every time I see the highlights of the pre-game Senior Day, I get that special feeling," Brown said. "It is one of the most moving things I've ever been a part of. Everybody sensed at that moment that a truly special person had touched our lives, and knew it was time for us to let him go and move on with his life. It reminds us all of the obvious fact that in life there will be adversity. We can't live in some kind of cosmic vacuum where only good things always happen. Something bad happens to you, and you have to want to overcome the odds if you are driven to succeed."

Like Kenny, Mann was directed by the coaching and sports information staffs to look for the banners.

"Someone said, 'They made a huge banner; you have to get Kenny to see it—and you have to see it, too,' " Mann said. "I didn't understand what this had to do with me—it was Kenny's day, not mine. So we saw it and it said, 'Thank You Kenny and Mimi.' Emotionally, I was just on overload."

Appreciative of others' kind words for her efforts with Kenny, Mimi Mann said Walker—and Osborne—were the ones who set the whole stage for the incredible success story that was to follow.

"I don't think I had a part in any of the success he had," Mann said. "It was excellent that he could have the same employee working with him. That was more efficient, having a consistent person. It didn't have to be me—anyone could have been selected. The key was that the University of Nebraska was smart enough to have an interpreter from the get-go, and they kept the same person."

Walker's teammate and roommate, Jon Crippen, also holds that memory near his heart.

"That was awesome," Crippen said. "That was probably the most touching moment I have ever experienced. You have to understand what it is like at Memorial Stadium. Even when I wasn't sniffing any game time my first year, just to run out on that field with 76,000 fans screaming and shaking the place was awesome. But that last day, there were 76,000 not making a peep with all of their hands up in the air in deaf applause. And then Kenny ran out there by himself. He had felt the vibration of the stadium before, but never heard the applause. That day, he heard the applause. It was all for him."

Likewise, linebacker Pat Tyrance still gets goosebumps thinking about that moment.

"It was a great moment in humanity for Kenny's efforts and his contribution to the state and the university," Tyrance said. "Kenny showed a great amount of love and respect for Nebraska. I'm grateful I was there that day."

Walker usually does not take time to think about all the things he misses out on because of his deafness. However, that day is among the times he wished he could have taken in the entire aura from a different perspective.

"I wish I could have hearing for just one day to hear that noise when they come out the tunnel," Kenny said with a smile. "I could sense as a freshman running out that it was something special. It was an experience I could never have imagined. I could feel the vibration of the stadium in my shoulder pads, and I could feel the beat of the drum from the band."

As fans continued to wave as Walker walked out of the stadium for the final time as a player, Walker felt a football-sized lump in his throat.

"It was so hard to leave the field that day," Walker said. "Nebraska gave me so many opportunities, most of which had nothing to do with football."

That day—and the memory of it—represented a lot of things that Kenny meant to his friends. The deafness, while the reason for the affectionate effort of the Husker fans, wasn't the whole story of Kenny Walker.

"One thing you have to understand is that Kenny was the type of person who would have been memorable if he wasn't deaf, or if he had never played football," Tyrance said. "The hearing impairment made him that much more special. Had he not been deaf, I don't know if he would have the amount of sensitivity and drive and focus to really serve others—which is just an example of how he turned something that could be negative into something very positive for not just himself, but hundreds, and even thousands of people. He is the kind of person who looks to take someone facing a challenge under his wing and give them tutelage whereas other people might disregard that kind of person because of the commitment it takes."

Crippen also remembers more than just a "deaf football player."

"He wanted to be the best at everything," Crippen said. "I don't think it was a case where he wanted to be better than everyone else—he just wanted to be the best he could be. I have to admit that his drive shocked me. I was as disciplined as anybody, but I learned as much as anyone did from Kenny Walker. He would push me so much when we worked out together. Since we both played defense, he would push me in practice. The guy isn't just a great athlete, he's stronger than a horse."

Husker quarterback Gerry Gdowski thinks of Walker's impact on the program and all the people he affected during his five years in Lincoln.

"It's a great story about somebody who could overcome something and not let it hinder him in his quest for what he wanted to accomplish," Gdowski said. "A lot of people today can come up with a lot of excuses for why they can't do something. Kenny is a good example of someone who didn't let his circumstances determine his goals."

Coach Brown said everyone in the stadium had a great opportunity that day.

"The thing about the whole Kenny Walker story is that we can all take something from it into our own lives," Brown said. "You really missed the point if you couldn't apply what you saw in Kenny Walker to your own life. He certainly is one of the most inspirational people you could ever imagine meeting. He inspired me. Something else that he did, because of his determination and the kind of character he demonstrated, was he pulled everyone around him to do remarkable things. Coach McBride learned sign language. You saw people stepping up and going above what they normally thought they could do. To me that is the true test of inspiration—not one who just inspires themselves but who also inspires those around them."

Assistant coach Milt Tenopir, who recruited Kenny to Nebraska, said Walker set high goals, and the honor of Academic All-Conference told Tenopir that Walker could do whatever he wanted in life.

"The fact that Kenny accomplished so many things that hearing people did not accomplish really says something about him," Tenopir said.

What Walker brought to the team, Brown believes, couldn't be gauged with a tape measure or stopwatch.

"You can measure remarkable athletic ability and strength," Brown said. "But it is hard to measure the heart. What Kenny had in his heart was contagious. He had to overcome so many things that we take for granted. Yet, he was so focused, so intense that he was able to keep the perspective and attitude he needed to achieve what he did at Nebraska."

Osborne also appreciated Walker's efforts.

"I know, particularly for people who have hearing loss, that a lot of people took encouragement from what Kenny was able to do," Osborne said. "He served as a great role model, particularly to people who have a hearing problem to overcome."

Through Walker, Tyrance said, people—especially in the stadium that day—had an opportunity to find that they had more in common than they might realize.

"That's what makes him special," Tyrance said. "When you personally experience a degree of challenge, such as being deaf, it enables you to cross different gaps and bridges between other people. Things we would see as differences, Kenny saw as potential for other areas of strength. Kenny was able to use his experience, and that enabled him to be more sensitive and to not be concerned with outward appearances. Kenny has always been able to see individuals for who they are."

Like other coaches and players, Walker's message had a lot more to do with life than football for Tyrance.

"Kenny was truly an inspiration for a lot of the players—and for anyone who was around him," Tyrance said. "You truly had a sense of what a special gift he was, not just as an athlete, but as a person."

In addition to Walker, many other players respected the way Osborne supported Walker.

"I have a great deal of respect and love for Coach Osborne," Tyrance said from Massachusetts where he is finishing his residency as a medical doctor. "I am commonly asked here about my experience at Nebraska and Coach Osborne, and I have nothing but good things to say about Coach and the school. I was not surprised at the relationship Kenny and Coach Osborne had. Coach Osborne is a great human being, a father figure and a person with great character. Coach Osborne also pushes and drives himself, like Kenny does. So in recruiting Kenny, perhaps Coach Osborne saw bringing him along as a challenge to himself. Coach Osborne is so much into developing great people, not football players. In order to survive outside of football, Coach Osborne used to say, you have to be well-rounded. I don't think when Coach Osborne saw Kenny that he focused on his hearing as much as other coaches would have. Coach Osborne just saw the potential Kenny had as a person, and I believe that's what appealed to Coach Osborne, as was the case with all the players Coach Osborne recruited."

Osborne retired at the end of the 1997 season after winning his third national championship over the final four years as the Husker's coach. During the ceremony honoring Osborne in the spring of 1998, messages from a few former players were played on the HuskerVision. One of those was from Walker, who thanked

Osborne for believing in him and giving him the opportunity and support to help Walker make a life of his own.

"I always liked Kenny," Osborne said. "He's always had a great heart. He seemed to be a guy who cared about the program and other people. He worked really hard to overcome whatever communication problem he had. He was a real asset."

Walker was sad to see Osborne retire because he knew what a great influence Osborne had been on thousands of young men. At the same time, Walker knew Osborne had earned the right to have his life back after so many 12-18 hour days at the football complex.

"Coach Osborne coached for something like 35 years," Kenny said. "He worked with thousands of players and won three national championships as a head coach, so he deserves time to just be happy with his family."

Osborne, a devout Christian who was never too high or too low emotionally, admitted he was touched on Senior Day, 1990.

"I always knew where I stood with Kenny because he was prone to be more demonstrative with his feelings," Osborne said. "I always knew we had a great relationship. I always think about Kenny. He is a great guy who means a lot to me."

CHAPTER 12

DRAFTED

After playing in the Senior Bowl, Kenny was getting good reviews about his draft status from NFL scouts. However, at the NFL Combine in Indianapolis in March, where the top college players are tested by professional scouts, Kenny was not in top shape because he was working hard on schoolwork.

"They expected me to be a third-round pick," Walker said. "But because of the deafness and my weight, there were some concerns. Plus, I didn't really help myself at the NFL Combine. I was so busy with school that I wasn't as focused as I could have been on the Combine. That might have hurt me a bit. I gained 10 pounds when the season ended."

On draft day 1991, Walker waited and waited to no avail. Out in Denver, Colorado, the Broncos' first-round pick, Husker linebacker Mike Croel, was answering questions about Walker.

"It is a fact that the reason I was drafted by the Broncos had a lot to do with Mike Croel, who spoke to Dan Reeves the night before the second day of the draft," Kenny said.

Dan Reeves, the coach of the Broncos at that time, said Croel wholeheartedly endorsed Walker to the Broncos.

"Mike said, 'Coach, we never had a problem with him at Nebraska. He always did what he was supposed to do,'" Reeves said. "You saw that on film. Of course, a player doesn't get to be an All-American if he's not doing what he's supposed to do. We thought he could have been some kind of linebacker in the NFL if he could hear. But there are so many formations and stuff with people changing places. There are some plays where you line up as the weakside linebacker, but then the formation changes and you are the strongside linebacker that play. There is a lot of communication that goes on verbally on defense."

Walker knew he had other factors working against him besides his deafness. The most glaring one was that Walker wasn't big enough to be a defensive lineman.

"I was happy to get the call the day of the draft," Kenny said. "I was getting worried because we were in the eighth round, and they hadn't called my name. I thought I was going to be a third-round pick. To drop to the eighth round was disappointing. Plus, my weight—being too small to be a true lineman—was against me, too. Denver called me and said they were going to draft me. But by then I had become despondent, so I left and went fishing. I caught several fish that day. Anyway, I came back from fishing and everyone told me that I had been drafted by the Denver Broncos. Since I had lived in Denver, it was very, very exciting."

Despite the obvious geographic connection, the Broncos weren't Walker's favorite team. In fact, Reeves was once a player for Walker's all-time favorite NFL team.

"I was a Cowboys fan," Kenny said. "Tony Dorsett was my favorite player."

In Reeves, Walker found a coach who seemed similar to Osborne in a lot of ways.

"I remember when I got the call from Coach Reeves," Kenny said. "Dan Reeves said, 'Welcome to Denver, Kenny. We're glad to have you. We'll teach you in mini-camp, and then you'll be on your way.' Dan Reeves was the easiest coach to get along with."

While Walker was glad to join the Broncos, he never really considered Denver a possibility. He thought any team drafting him would have a four-man front line.

"I hadn't considered the possibility of the Broncos drafting me," Kenny said. "I was expecting to go to an NFC team. I really wanted to go to the Minnesota Vikings. I liked their program, and they had good coaches. I always liked Minnesota because of the four-man rush. But I was just glad to have the chance."

Husker linebacker Pat Tyrance, who was drafted in the eighth round by the Los Angeles Rams, said Walker should have gone in the top four rounds.

"If he could hear, he would have gone earlier in the draft, I believe," Tyrance said. "At least that's my opinion, that some teams were scared, or fearful, of drafting him, that they did not have the patience to work with him."

Kenny's future father-in-law, Dan Offenburger, thought Kenny would go sooner in the draft.

"I knew he had put up a great senior year," Offenburger said. "I was a little disappointed he went that late, but you can see where teams thought the deafness might be a problem. He went through a similar thing with being recruited out of high school. When the draft was on, I just kept thinking, 'I hope they give him a chance.' "

It might seem logical that Kenny would have a difficult time moving on from Lincoln. He had grown in a stable environment while at Nebraska and had a good support system. However, Walker claims he was more than ready for the new surroundings and challenges.

"Ironically, it wasn't that hard to leave Nebraska when I was drafted by the NFL because while I knew I would miss Lincoln, I knew I had worked for the opportunity of playing in the NFL, and now—just like I had at Nebraska—I had to make the most of it," Kenny said. "And moving on is just part of becoming a man."

Although Kenny had lived in Denver from the time he was in kindergarten until the family moved back to Texas for Kenny's high school years, the mile-high altitude took a toll on him when he reported to the Broncos.

"When I arrived at mini-camp, I ran one lap before I was out of breath. I couldn't believe how thin the air was," Kenny said. "So I worked hard in training camp to get myself in shape. Unfortunately, I pulled my hamstring and that forced me to rest for three weeks. Eventually, I worked really hard and ended up making the team."

Since Mimi Mann lived in Lincoln, the Broncos solicited the services of another interpreter. Guy Smith was working in the city of Greeley, northeast of Denver on the plains, when he heard about the job opportunity.

"Someone from the Broncos called and said they needed an interpreter for training camp," Guy said. "It was just a one-day deal, from what I understood, where I would interview for the job. I got down there and met the general manager, John Beake, and there was just a huge stack of resumes on his desk to sign for this deaf player they had drafted."

Smith knew the competition for the job would be intense. So he turned from interpreter to salesman, pitching himself to Beake in every possible manner.

"I really tried to sell myself to him," Guy said. "I told him that I loved the job and that I was perfect for it. My family had a block of 22 season tickets in the south stands at Mile High since the franchise was in Denver. I had been a huge Broncos fan my whole life—I thought that would help. I knew my signing skills were good, too. I told him I'd move to Denver if I got the job, so I'd always be nearby."

Mimi Mann was at the Broncos' training complex when Kenny and Guy first met.

"It's really important that I have someone who understands me," Kenny told Guy.

"I understand you just fine," Guy answered.

Kenny then said something else.

"What?" Guy asked. "You lost me."

Guy said the situation was comical because he had just assured Kenny in the previous statement that he understood him so well.

"I didn't understand his following statement at all," Guy said. "I felt bad because I had just told him I understood him perfectly. But it was more funny than anything else. I live by my heart, and so does Kenny. So in that regard, right away we connected. From the first day, it worked out. Mimi was planning to be there the whole day, to ease the transition. By midway through the day, Kenny told her that I would be fine.

"As an interpreter I'm only there because there was a deaf guy, I wasn't there for my football knowledge," Guy said. "I didn't have time to be star-struck. It was like meeting John Elway—the first time I met him, he was naked in the locker room. He said, 'Hi, nice to meet you.' He seemed like a nice guy, but it was a business thing when I worked there. It wasn't the kind of situation where I could have felt free to ask him for an autograph."

During a meal at the team's training camp in Greeley in August of 1991, Kenny was sitting with Guy and several other players. Kenny noticed a player a few tables over who was mouthing the word, "choking."

The player, Matt McCall, a rookie free agent offensive lineman from Texas A&M, was getting funny looks from everyone else at his table. But since he wasn't getting any air to his lungs, he couldn't make a sound. Since no one else read lips, Walker was the only one who picked up on what McCall was trying to say. So Kenny rushed over to the table and stood behind McCall, applying the Heimlich maneuver. The piece of meat was dislodged, and a shaken but otherwise all-right McCall thanked Walker.

"Matt was really choking at the point Kenny got to him," Smith said. "I don't know if you could say he was dying, but he wasn't getting any air into his system, and from what I understand, that can cause death—so it would not be a stretch to say Kenny saved Matt's life. Kenny just got up and cleared it out of him."

Walker wasn't phased by the moment. He came back to the table, sat next to Guy, and took another bite of eggs and sausage.

"Everyone was like, 'Wow,' because they realized that a special person had just done something very special," Smith said. "Kenny, on the other hand, came back to our table and just sat down, getting right back in the conversation. Kenny was simply not the kind of person who would say, 'Look what I did.' People were coming by, patting Kenny on his back and telling him what a good thing he had done. Kenny just smiled and said, 'thank you' to everyone who stopped."

Reeves, a Christian man, said Walker was in the training room's food area that day near McCall for a reason.

"I have always believed that if you were challenged in one area, God made up for it in other places," Reeves said. "Kenny's other senses are so much greater than hearing people's are. So while it was a big deal—especially to Matt, of course—it didn't surprise me that Kenny Walker stepped up and maybe saved a guy's life. Kenny was always paying attention to things in whatever he was doing. He'd read lips wherever he was, which tuned him in to some things that others around him were not aware of. That's what happened in the lunch room that day."

Wade Phillips, the defensive coordinator for Denver at the time, said everyone was impressed with Walker's poise.

"I was there at the time—and it really was that amazing," Phillips said. "There aren't really words for what Kenny did. I think everybody was excited about Kenny and for Kenny. He showed what people can do when they are driven. I feel that all of us have handicaps, but in a game like professional football, it is really hard for someone with that kind of handicap. That's one of the reasons we were all so proud of him."

Walker liked a lot about the NFL. After surviving on a shoestring budget in Lincoln, Kenny found the NFL pay scale much to his liking.

"It's amazing when you get the first check," Kenny said. "I didn't put it in the bank. Marti had to help me deposit it. I grew up under relatively meager means."

Another shock came on the first play of the Broncos' first exhibition game.

"The first play of the first game in the preseason, we were playing against the Detroit Lions in the Hall of Fame Game in Canton, Ohio," Kenny said. "I was right in the middle of the field on the kickoff. I remember like it was yesterday. Someone hit me. His hand went right through the facemask. When I opened my eyes, I had double vision—actually it was triple vision. I was walking funny, and I could barely see. I took my helmet off and looked around, and there was blood everywhere.

"I was bleeding pretty badly," Kenny said. "I looked at the trainer and said, 'I will be needing a little help to get to the locker room.' They took me to the locker room and got the cut closed, and I came back and played. I had to—I was so mad."

Walker made the team and saw extended playing time on special teams, serving as a backup on the defensive line.

"I had a decent rookie year," Kenny said. "The coaches were impressed with how I was doing on the defensive line. And I was doing all right on the special teams. I would have liked to be starting, but it was the NFL, so I was just happy to be playing."

The media really jumped on Kenny's story. The sight of Guy signing to Kenny on the sidelines during the game made for great footage to go along with Kenny's inspirational stories. Since there were no other deaf players in the league, Kenny became a role model for not just deaf people, but anyone facing a handicap.

"One of the public relations people with the Broncos told me that Kenny was the first member of the team to ever get more mail, interview requests and requests for public appearances than Elway," Smith said. "It never bothered Kenny at all to make time for people. Even when we'd be out eating in the middle of a meal and someone would want to talk to him or get an autograph, Kenny was more than eager to accommodate them."

Kenny remembers one interview in particular.

"Kenny, what is the stupidest question someone has ever asked you?" the writer asked.

"I guess it's this one: 'Can you drive a car?' " Kenny responded.

The writer laughed. "Someone actually thought you could drive a car!"

After letting the writer enjoy a full guffaw, Kenny explained that he was a very competent, safe driver.

Kenny welcomed the intelligent questions. Although he was accommodating to all interviewers, he grew tired of answering some of the same questions over and over.

"Being around the NFL media was more involved than at Nebraska," Kenny said. "They ask you the same question over and over. You get tired of it. I wasn't always sure if they wanted to talk to me because I was deaf or if it was because I was a football player."

"The most common question was, 'If you could change and become hearing, would you?' " Kenny recalls.

And his answer?

"I said, 'No. Why would I do that? This is what God planned for me. I am on the way; I am on the path. It's not an easy way for me, but it's my way,' " Walker said.

"He was just so accommodating with the media, and most of the coverage was quite good," Martina Walker said. "He wanted to help the cause for deaf people, and no matter what the request was—for an interview or a public appearance—Kenny just couldn't say no."

He gave reporters his story but was never able to tell his whole story—which is one of the reasons he decided to do this book.

"It was frustrating because I couldn't explain [to the reporters] what happened to me through the years," Kenny said. "I don't have the ability to tell my story because I can't make the words the way I need to—I have to use the interpreter. So I did what I could for those who are in the deaf community. I hope I helped a little because that really was one of my goals."

Wade Phillips, defensive coordinator for the Broncos, was in the locker room and on the practice field during several of the interviews Walker gave in his two years as a Bronco.

"I think he answered the same question a million times," Phillips said. "Yet, he was always very gracious. He was excited about being there. A lot of kids were looking at him. Not just handicapped kids but kids everywhere. He knew he was a role model to a lot of folks in a lot of different circumstances, and he handled it as well as anyone could have ever hoped."

One thing that Walker's former teammates, coaches and friends on the Broncos remember is that Walker never wanted anything other players didn't get.

"What you have to understand about Kenny is that he never sought any special treatment," Smith said. "To him, being a deaf football player was no different from being any other kind of football player. He told me, 'In football, you tackle the guy who has the ball whether you can hear or not. It's the same rules for everyone.' That's a good way to look at it. Because to Kenny, deafness wasn't an issue."

Walker's battle for independence once got Smith's toes inadvertently stepped on by Walker's wife, Martina.

"I got upset and had to talk to Guy once," Martina said. "What happened was Guy was standing behind Kenny on the sideline during the game, and the coach came up to Kenny—so I was thinking, 'Why doesn't Guy get up in front of Kenny? That is his job!' I went down and pulled Guy aside and really let my opinion be known. I told him, 'Your job is to interpret.' He let me finish what I had to say and then answered, 'Kenny told me to stand behind him.' I realized Kenny wanted to be independent. He does not want to be babysat. At the same time, I knew he needed Guy for information. But apparently Kenny told Guy, 'Stand behind me. I will call you when I need you.' I can see Kenny's point."

Reeves appreciated Walker's attitude in regard to eschewing any special treatment.

"Kenny didn't want anything special made out of him being unable to hear," Reeves said. "He never wanted to be treated differently. He wanted to keep moving forward with his life. We had to do some things differently, and we had Guy and some others pick up some sign language. But what made it work was that Kenny never quit on himself or his teammates. He was just a great competitor."

Professional football opened a lot of doors for Kenny—one was that he made a lot of friends.

"I liked a lot of the players I met that first year, like Karl Mecklenburg," Walker said. "And Simon Fletcher was a great guy who I liked a lot. I also started to get close to Ron Holmes and Alphonso Carreker, who were both defensive linemen, but both were traded or released while I was there. That was hard to deal with. At Nebraska you got at least a few years with the guys around you, with the exception of the seniors, of course. You don't expect that when you first get to the NFL—to have friends one day who are gone the next. But it happens, so you deal with it."

Even during training camp, Kenny insisted on being treated like the other rookies when the veterans started the initiation rituals.

"During camp, they made all the rookies stand up and sing a song," Martina said. "I understand it is supposed to embarrass the rookies. Not Kenny. He loves to sing. He will ask me, 'Do you think I am a good singer?' He's always singing around the house."

Still, it was apparent early on that the NFL was a business.

"In professional football, it's go, go and go; you have to move faster, and you can't waste any time," Walker said. "It is a business whereas in college the emphasis was on learning and continuous improvement, even on the football field. In pro football the guys are smart and strong. You have to be smart and be a great athlete just to be on the field. You have to use good judgment, especially against the better players. It's a lot of fundamental work. But it's not a sport the way it is in college. It's like a business, and the field is like a factory."

The Broncos fell just short of their goal to play in the 1992 Super Bowl.

"The first year ended on a rough note because we really thought we'd make it to the Super Bowl, but we lost in the last seconds to the Buffalo Bills," Kenny said. "And it was our own fault because we made a lot of mistakes."

Still, Denver finished the year at 12-4 before losing 10-7 to the Bills in the AFC Championship Game, despite holding Jim Kelly,

Andre Reed, Thurman Thomas and the rest of the Bills' high-powered offense to only 213 yards of total offense.

Kenny's first year personally ended on a high note. He was voted by his teammates as the winner of the 1991 Bob Peck Award, given to the most inspirational player.

The Broncos offered a summer workout program. Walker enjoyed every repetition of every workout.

Former Bronco Simon Fletcher's most memorable moment with Walker came after Walker's rookie season ended.

"It was during the off-season conditioning," Fletcher said. "I was always trying to get people motivated to run harder and lift weights harder because I knew that would determine how our team would do the following season—it really set the tone for the coming season. One day I was in the weight room, and I didn't feel like being there. We were seven weeks into the off-season program, so I was content that day to just go through the motions and get it done. Of course Kenny noticed that right away and made a motion toward me. I said, 'What does that mean?' Kenny came up to me and said, 'Let's go! Get busy! No slacking off, there's only six more weeks until training camp!' That right there is what Kenny Walker stands for to me."

Fletcher claims Walker affected his life far more than just in regard to football.

"You have to draw incredible strength from him because he never let his handicap stop him from putting forth his maximum effort," Fletcher said. "He should be viewed as a shining example that anyone can do anything. It would have been easy so many times for him to give up—like in high school, or at Nebraska. He could have said, 'I just can never be good enough because I can't hear or speak normally.' But he found out where he could compensate, and pushed himself."

Walker's story made for good headlines and footage, but after seeing Walker's work ethic, Fletcher knew Walker could accomplish whatever he wanted to.

"It did not surprise me that he made the team," Fletcher said. "And it didn't surprise me that he ended up starting his second year. One of the things coaches in the NFL love is players who never quit because there are players who take a play off here and there. Kenny was the kind who was going to go all out every play. That is a big part of who he is as a person. So I think I was most impressed with his effort. Every play to Kenny was the most important play in the biggest game of his life. And his strength was phenomenal."

Walker's businesslike approach was akin to Fletcher's.

"I see similarities between Kenny and myself," Fletcher said. "I was there for a specific reason, just as Kenny was, and that was to play football and help my team win. I posted some good statistics but didn't get a lot of accolades for it, which did not bother me. Any accolade would be great, don't get me wrong, but I was not there for that. That's how Kenny was; he was not there to be a 'deaf football player.' He was there to compete and work as hard as he could to help his team win."

Fletcher never ceased to be amazed by the academic accomplishments Walker earned at Nebraska.

"For him to work hard enough to be Academic All-Conference...well, it says that he's a lot smarter than I am," Fletcher said with a smile. "Once again, that's just Kenny Walker saying, 'Give me an opportunity, and I will take care of business.' The only thing that made Kenny different from anyone else as far as what they could do, was that Kenny was deaf. But in every other way, Kenny is everyone else's equal."

Walker found starting for Denver his second year a double-edged sword; that is, to move into the starting lineup, someone else was moved out—like out of town and off the team.

"The way I became a starter was a good news/bad news thing," Kenny said. "Ron Holmes was a good friend of mine, and they got rid of him. That's how I became a starter. Should I have been happy to be a starter or sad to see a good friend—a nice man and a great player—go? You feel a little of both, and it is confusing."

So even though he was starting, he was growing less content with his life in the NFL.

"The second season was awful," Kenny said. "Even though I was doing better and starting, football was not fun anymore. I didn't stay for the money. I was thinking about asking to be traded because I didn't like working for the Broncos. But they had done so much for me, especially Coach Reeves."

Although the Broncos didn't have a great season on the field, going 8-8, in the 1992 off-season, Walker was honored with the prestigious Most Courageous Athlete Award from the Philadelphia Sportswriters Association, and he testified before Congress on behalf of the National Institute on Deafness and Other Communication Disorders.

Heading into his third training camp with the Broncos, Walker felt like he was improving even though defensive line coach Ernie Stautner was riding him hard.

With the constant criticism from Stautner, Walker had a feeling he wasn't going to make the team.

"I was—and remain—a big fan of the Denver Broncos, and I always will be," Guy Smith said. "But what happened was Ernie Stautner thought that if you couldn't hear, it meant you were stupid. Yet, the other coaches could understand Kenny. But Ernie was from the old school—he must have been about 68 when Kenny was there. He was constantly on Kenny and constantly on me. What happened was that Ernie did not believe Kenny could do the job because he could not hear. That's what it came down to."

The problem between Stautner and Walker, Smith believes, had nothing to do with football. Rather, Smith felt Stautner would not work to bridge the communication gap.

"That's what killed me with the whole Ernie Stautner stuff," Smith said. "He thought Kenny was stupid and treated him terribly. He brought Kenny down every day. Never once did Kenny stand up and back talk him, even though I would have. It was a terribly hard time for Kenny. The other players knew Kenny was a good player."

Walker's father-in-law, Dan Offenburger, said he had a feeling Walker wasn't in the Broncos' plans as the 1992 season wound down.

"The wheels were starting to come off at the end of his second season," Offenburger said. "Dan Reeves was under pressure, and it was pretty obvious he was going to be gone at the end of the year. All the support and consideration would leave with Dan. Certainly, Kenny was good enough to play and be an outstanding player if he had Charlie McBride or Tom Osborne coaching him. I just don't see how, ranking Kenny against the other players they had, they could cut him. It was obvious to me that they just didn't want him there. But it would have been kinder to cut him right away, so he could have signed and gone to the beginning of another team's training camp."

Smith also could sense Walker's tenure in Denver was coming to an end, especially after Reeves was not offered a contract after the 1992 season.

"If Dan Reeves was still coaching in Denver, Kenny would still be playing there today," Smith said. "One of the coaches came up to me near the end of Kenny's time there and said, 'Don't tell anyone I told you this, or I will have to deny it or get fired, but it was the luck of the draw that Kenny got Ernie as a coach. If he had one of us, we'd make it work.' I believe that to this day if Kenny had Mike Nolan or Charlie Waters as his position coach, he would have not only made the team, but he would have continued to get better and the communication problem might have gone away to the point that my role was limited. As every day passed, the communication improved, except with Ernie, of course."

Smith said an irony he found was that after working two years with Kenny, he could understand Kenny—even without Kenny signing—better than Smith could other linemen.

"That's one thing that it took a while for people to realize," Smith said. "The funniest thing I discovered is that all defensive linemen are hard to understand."

Still, heading into training camp in 1993, Walker felt good. And when he made it all the way to when there was only one cut remaining, he started to think that he had a shot.

He was wrong.

"I went in with a good perspective for my third year," Kenny said. "I had worked hard in the off-season. I made it down to the final cut, and then I was released. I didn't even think that was a possibility because I had been starting. On the way home in the truck that day, I cried. I couldn't understand what happened. I was working so hard. It was there—I was so close to succeeding."

Offenburger wrote a letter to Denver owner Pat Bowlen after Walker was released. Bowlen personally responded.

September 19, 1993

TO: Mr. Pat Bowlen
FROM: Dan Offenburger
RE: Kenny Walker

Mr. Bowlen, I am Kenny Walker's father-in-law. I may be a meddling old fool, but I have some thoughts on his situation that I would like for you to consider. Kenny has no idea that I am writing this. If it is worthwhile, use it. If not, please excuse me for bothering you.

I am the former athletic director at Creighton University where I was on the staff for seventeen years. In my current position I am working on a project with six national organizations for the physically disabled in sports. I really think I am writing less on behalf of Kenny and more for my grandson Tommy (Kenny's six-year-old deaf stepson) and millions of other kids. It may be that this "food for thought" is of value to you, the Broncos and Kenny.

I would like to have written this to Coach Wade Phillips and his staff, but I can imagine their schedule during the season limits time spent on the type of reflection that I am suggesting.

I am aware that your team has lost, temporarily, the services of Greg Kragen and Dan Williams. I assume this is complicated by the to-be-expected nuisance injuries, such as those suffered this year by Willie Oshidan and Daren Drozdov. Your team needs backup support, or at least access to it.

From the outside, it appears your team will not at this time bring back Kenny. Based upon my experience in athletics and in communications, I would assume a decision has been made that he is marginal at best in ability. Beyond that, I deduct that the extra effort required in communications adds a factor against the idea of bringing him back.

From this basic view, I offer these thoughts:

1. Kenny reached a point similar to this after about two years at the University of Nebraska. He was not finding a place to play, and he (and I assume, the staff) experienced frustration that affected performance. He almost dropped out of school. Nebraska stayed with Kenny. It had the numbers of players and time to invest, which is not the situation of an NFL team. Kenny stayed, also. The mutual investment of school and athlete paid off when he became an All-American and a person who was and is highly marketable for the school. Beyond that, it produced a great benefit for the 43,000,000 disabled persons of this nation and for the millions of fans who grew to admire Kenny's role model status. I wonder if there is not cause to consider whether similar developments are still possible on the NFL level.

2. Kenny has at least two major limitations as an NFL player. He is the wrong size for the positions he has played. He is deaf, which apparently keeps him from playing the positions which would better fit his size. In stature and talents, if he were not deaf, he might well be a star linebacker or perhaps even a receiver. That is said with the thought in mind that he played at 235 pounds at Nebraska, was extremely quick and fast, and had the athletic skills best indicated by his high school background as an all-state basketball player (as well as football and track). I spoke on one occasion to his college position coach, who did not feel Kenny could play linebacker. Kenny still thinks he could play linebacker, though he is certainly willing to play other positions.

3. In 1991, as a rookie, Kenny added weight to 250 pounds. He retained most of his quickness, had 5.5 sacks, was a member of special teams, could be seen constantly hustling on pursuit, and seemed (from the outside) to have positive character and attitude. He also seemed to enjoy playing, as reflected by his disposition on the field.

4. In 1992, Kenny started 15 of 16 games, missing only the Houston game when the defense was altered against the "run and shoot" offense. But he then weighed 260 pounds, had problems with his feet,

seemed slowed in movement, ceased to be as prevalent in pursuit and pass rushing. His lack of sacks, however, may also have been due in part to his not being used in most passing situations. What became apparent to those familiar with the communication problems involved, however, was the growing evidence of his frustration (and that of his coaches). This was a player who had "lost his spark." When I was in Denver last October for the birth of his son Bo, I noted a marked change in Kenny's situation with the Broncos. By the way, by then he was no longer a factor as a special teams player.

5. In pre-season 1993, Kenny had added weight to 274, was dropped to a reserve role, was utilized as a nose tackle, grew obviously more frustrated, experienced further frustration on the part of his coaches and ultimately was waived. But one contention by many familiar with the communications challenges involved is that this all is more likely a result of communications, rather than a matter of talent. (However, I realize it is also possible that if the communications problems were solved, he could still fall short of standards.)

6. Part of the problem, I think, has to do with the weight issue. I really lack the knowledge of NFL football to make such a judgment. Some whose opinion on football I respect feel Kenny should be able to play with some or all of the additional weight. Others similarly qualified have the opinion that his optimal weight is somewhere in the 240 to 250 pound range. I note that the Broncos frequently use linebackers in the 235 to 240 range as pass rushers. As I have watched Kenny's decline in status, I have often wondered how slashing and effective he would be at that size, for that is how he most excelled in college. Is that another Mecklenburg or Fletcher now gone to waste? At that size, he most likely would be an excellent special teams player. Time would tell whether he would be effective against the rush if he weighed less. Or, he might be able to carry the extra weight.

7. But the issue to which I can add insight, I hope, is that of communication. Years ago, I first faced the problem of communicating across culture gaps when I worked with black youth in an urban setting. I am white. A few years later, I worked closely with highly-educated

Vietnamese physicians and their families. I found myself as exhausted and frustrated by the experience with the Vietnamese doctors as I had been with the black ghetto kids. I finally decided that the similarity in my feelings during those two occasions was because I am from a white and middle-class background, which was in stark contrast to that of both poor blacks and well-to-do Vietnamese. I began to grow in both situations and found the return on my efforts to be a highlight of my life. In recent years I have worked a good deal with several disabled groups, including the deaf. I found the same frustration and the accompanying limitations and unproductive developments from the relationships until I realized that once again this comes from dealing across the culture gap. Once I realized this, I relaxed and have taken an entirely new approach with the deaf. I still experience problems, but the communication is there, and the great rewards from such a relationship is the result. Instead of being a major aggravation, in all three experiences (black youth, Vietnamese doctors, deaf citizens), the positive experience is a thrill.

8. I think there are steps the Broncos can take that will make it beneficial to bring back Kenny, be it as immediate help to overcome the injury losses, in a developmental role on the reserve squad or in a non-playing role with the Broncos or the NFL. If I think I can add insight for your staff on this matter, I can only guess that expertise is out there for the asking.

The Nebraska coaches would be invaluable. Perhaps one of the foremost advisors would be Dr. Larry Fleischer, a deaf college professor and President of the American Athletic Association for the Deaf (part of the U.S. Olympic structure). Through Dr. Fleischer, you can be put in touch with countless other resources. One person who can give you immediate insight is Jan Wilson, director for disabled sports at USOC headquarters in Colorado Springs. (Ask her about the experience of the deaf USA Team Handball athlete, once the obstacles to his progress were removed.) I imagine that your coaches, and perhaps you also, feel you have exhausted all possibilities. I cannot be certain, but I think you have only begun to scratch the surface of what is possible. This has not been because of a bad attitude or lack of ability by anyone. Your organization is, after all, the one which gave Kenny his chance.

9. Why try again? That is a good question. Any person knowledgeable of the issues involved can understand why NFL coaches in the midst of the season may shy from this. They have "a full platter" of problems already. But, Mr. Bowlen, this is something that is so important to our nation that it cries for the attention of you, your coaches and the NFL. What has happened with Kenny is what happens to deaf (and other disabled) school children when they matriculate in educational or employment systems which give up before the ultimate solution is found. It is what happens in society when deaf (and other disabled) adults become wards of government because career opportunities are not developed. So much talent is wasted. So much cost is incurred by a society that supports these people and their families. This is so vital as a social issue that the NFL might well be advised to give the Broncos an extra roster spot (not in the top 47) for a year or two, just to show our 43 million disabled persons we are trying. Do not give Kenny anything. Do not keep him on the team if he cannot play at the level. He doesn't deserve that and would not want it. But consider renewing the effort (with the help of those who understand and can help develop different approaches) to discover what he can learn.

10. Reflect for a moment on what is going on in the minds of Kenny, those close to him and the millions who see him as a role model. The plight of such persons (be it getting in the correct school situation, getting a laboring job or making the team...elementary, college, Olympics, NFL, whatever...) is an aggravation dilemma. Sometimes there is rage, a desire to fight, to be a strong advocate. Sometimes there is shyness, a desire not to be a problem, a willingness to back away. Most of all there is the frustration of knowing what happens when the right answer is found and the success comes. That's what makes parents proud of the kid who becomes a good student. That's what drives the deaf (or other disabled) to be such over achievers when they finally find their niche. That's why Kenny became an All-American, rather than just another player at Nebraska.

11. I ask you to consider this an investment for your team. I think the Broncos have not had the resource expertise that will produce the correct coaches/player relationships. This is not because you don't care or don't have the ability. It is because the problem is far afield from the customary NFL routine. At least the Broncos cared enough to try it for two seasons. But if you and your staff step forward now, you may find immediate results in an experienced player on your squad. You may discover how well Kenny plays when the frustration and other communication inhibitors are taken away. You may discover how much he develops. (Though I have not the expertise to decide on the weight or positions issues, I think you may also discover great results when he plays at his optimal size.) Dallas may have been "America's team" at one point. The Chicago Cubs status and Atlanta Braves may have utilized nationwide TV exposure to achieve similar status. But that will pale compared to the loyalty you will attract if you make another investment of time, money and patience. Ask Nebraskans how Kenny is regarded in their state. Ask Dr. Fleischer and other leaders of the nation's deaf (and other disabilities) community. Our nation needs for you to make the attempt.

Mr. Bowlen, I have gone on far more than I had imagined. I hope you have taken time to read this. If you find it has merit, feel free to pass it on to your staff. At least, I have had the therapy of saying these things.

I have tried to write this letter as objectively as possible. But I am not objective in the case of Kenny Walker. As biased as I am on his behalf, I am convinced his case is a major issue in the lives of millions of Americans, the deaf and otherwise disabled. I really think my extensive background in intercollegiate athletics and with the nation's disabled has provided me with insight. I want you to consider this letter in a professional light.

It probably isn't fair, but you are in a unique spot in the United States. You have the opportunity to be the catalyst for wonderful developments for the nation's 43 million disabled. No one can rightly blame you if you wish you were not in this position. Yours is a very extra burden.

I understand you have the Jesuits in your background (Jake McGargill, a local businessman, was a classmate of your brother at Campion). So, too, have I been educated by and worked with the Jesuits. I don't agree with all they do. But I did learn from the Jesuits such ideas that one person can make a difference, it takes courage to step forward in leadership roles and we have a need for outstanding persons to take up the cause of the disadvantaged. In my opinion you and the Broncos have the opportunity either to step forward for the nation's disabled or to walk away. Along the way you may pick up one more excellent player, far beyond what happened with Kenny up to now. But you will be taking a major swing for 43 million people, including my grandson Tommy.

Thank you for your time and patience. Good luck this season and beyond. You, Coach Phillips and the staff have taken dramatic steps forward.

Dan Offenburger

September 21, 1993

Mr. Dan Offenburger
117 S. Elm
Shenandoah, Iowa 51601

Dear Dan:

Thank you for your kind letter concerning Kenny Walker. Throughout Kenny's career with the Broncos, I can say I was one of his strongest supporters. He brought many things to our football team, but perhaps the most important was his courage in the face of his handicap. This was a good lesson for the Broncos' management and the players. Unfortunately, football is a high paying entertainment business, and we are left very little room to treat it as only a game. Our coaching staff felt that Kenny's ability coupled with his handicap made it impossible for him to continue as a player.

My heart goes out to Kenny, and he knows my door is always open if there is any way I can help him with another career opportunity.

Yours truly,

Pat Bowlen

Guy Smith said other players were surprised to find out Walker was no longer a part of Denver's future.

"I had a coach and other linemen ask me why Ernie was always harassing Kenny," Guy said. "The other guys were genuinely inspired by Kenny's strength and ability—they told me this on more than one occasion."

Walker's good friend, Simon Fletcher, said Walker had the speed to play linebacker. Fletcher said Walker's status as the classic "Tweener"—a player who is too big to be a linebacker, but too small to be a defensive lineman—had a lot to do with how things turned out.

"There was just so much more talking at linebacker that it was a natural transition to play defensive line, especially with Kenny's reaction time and his speed," Fletcher said. "Throw in his strength, and he was a good defensive lineman. If he had been built to carry another 20 or 30 pounds, he would have been a Pro Bowl caliber player."

Reeves agreed, and thought that physically Walker had a lot of potential at linebacker had he been able to hear.

"He had the right size and speed for a linebacker, but the communication problem led him to the line, as it did at Nebraska," Reeves said. "We could always count on him. He made some unbelievable plays for us."

Still, Smith said he believes Walker left his mark on Denver, and the entire NFL as well. While Walker had plenty of talent and ability, Smith said it was Walker's inner strength that allowed him to succeed for those two years in Denver.

"You have to have athletic ability to make it in the league, but everyone who is on an NFL team has that ability," Smith said. "What made certain players better is they had heart. You just have to have heart."

A lot of the mail Walker received in Denver came from deaf people. But Smith said almost every single person could relate to Walker in one way or another.

"I view it differently than a lot of people do," Smith said. "I always viewed Kenny as not just a role model to deaf people, but to anyone with a challenge—the little boy who can't run as fast, or the girl who works hard to look nice, but just isn't pretty enough to draw attention at the prom. These people all have special qualities that they can use to overcome whatever they view as their shortcomings. That is what Kenny did. I don't even look at the football part of Kenny's life as the reason he succeeded. I see who he is and what he has become as a person as the reason he is a success."

The ending in Denver was not ideal, but Smith said the time he spent with Walker was memorable for a lot of reasons, not the least of which was Kenny's ability to make other people laugh, in addition to poking fun at himself.

"Once people learned he had a sense of humor, they found out how funny he was," Smith said. "And it worked the same way as Kenny got to know other players. Kenny just loved Shannon Sharpe, Denver's All-Pro tight end. In normal conversation Shannon swears more in one sentence than a sailor does in a day. Kenny loved for me to interpret Shannon because he was always laughing at what Shannon said. And Shannon is a very happy person, which appeals to Kenny."

Kenny was really into music, something Kenny's teammates knew from watching him move to the beat in the locker room. After practice one day, Guy took off as Kenny prepared to shower. Kenny really liked the beat of the CD playing, so he asked a teammate the name of the group. Kenny read his lips and went and bought the CD on the way home from practice. He picked Martina up in his truck and proudly turned up the volume and bass on his new CD.

The CD was by *2 Live Crew*, a rap band known for its songs about killing policemen and endorsing brutal violence toward women.

"Do you know what these words are?" Martina signed to Kenny.

Kenny shook his head sideways, indicating that he did not. Martina started interpreting the lyrics. Kenny covered his mouth in shock, grabbed the CD, and put it in the garbage. Martina was laughing as she saw Kenny's incredulous look.

"Dang, that's embarrassing!" Kenny said. "But I'm deaf. How am I supposed to know about the words? I just picked it because I liked the bass. I didn't know the words."

"He never listened to it again," Martina said.

"It's kind of bizarre," Martina said. "He's a really good dancer; he's into hip-hop a bit, BET, VH1 or MTV."

Another funny moment came when Kenny—who had a hard time saying no to any personal appearance request—showed up at a golf tourney.

"We went to a charity golf driving contest, and at that point, Kenny hadn't golfed before," Guy said. "It was a shot to make a hole in one on a short par 3, maybe 100 yards. Kenny asked what he should do. Someone handed him a club and said, 'Just hit the ball as hard as you can that way,' pointing toward the hole. Kenny hit the ball so hard it went almost 200 yards past the hole. Kenny said, 'That wasn't very hard.' I laughed and explained it more clearly. Everyone broke out laughing."

Kenny's wife remembers hearing Kenny's and Guy's collective adventures on road trips. Kenny always enjoyed meeting members of each town's deaf community.

"One time Kenny and the Broncos were playing the Bengals in Cincinnati," Martina said. "Guy and Kenny went to the motel. Whenever Kenny was on the road, it was common for deaf communities in each town to try and get ahold of Kenny. This man showed up and met Kenny and Guy. They hit it off right away, and he asked if he could take Kenny and Guy to dinner. They agreed, so they headed to the elevator. These teen age girls got in and saw the men signing back and forth. One said, 'Hey, look, these guys are deaf. We can say whatever we want.' They started saying some things that weren't very polite. The elevator stopped, and the girls motioned for the men to get out first. Guy turned around and said, 'Thanks. But you girls need to know that not everyone who signs is deaf.'"

Kenny also tried to introduce Smith to Kenny's favorite pastime, fishing.

"He gave me a fishing rod one time," Guy said. "He said, 'Here, have this one. It is nice. But I can't buy another one if I have this one. So if I give it to you, I can get another.' He was just such a good person."

Walker's former coach Dan Reeves said he still cherishes the time he had with Walker in Denver.

"I think I took from Kenny what everyone else did," Reeves said. "You see someone who has a handicap you can't imagine having yourself, and yet he lives his life like anyone else does. Without a doubt, I thought—and believe to this day—that bringing Kenny to Denver was worth it. Kenny is a really neat human being. And the guy had a great smile that could light up a room. He was a lot of fun to be around."

Like almost everyone else who came in contact with Walker, Smith learned a lot about himself during his time as Kenny's interpreter.

"I still think of Kenny often and hope he is well," Smith said. "I was reading something by Richard Bach, *Illusions*. It says, 'No one is ever given a dream without being given the power to make it come true.' To me, that is Kenny, and he is the perfect example of that. If you can dream it, you can do it. You can do anything. Just do it. Kenny lives that way, even today. He just won't let himself think 'I can't do this because I'm not good enough.' There's no question he is going to get there; the only real question is how he is going to get there."

Smith was very close to the Walker family.

"Guy was there when Bo was born, so he saw Bo being born," Martina said. "I had to have my uterus taken out during the birth because of the delivery. So we were spending time with my family and Guy, talking about Bo's birth, and my mom asked, 'What does a uterus look like?' Guy answered, 'Kind of like a roast.' Everyone started laughing. Guy was just great."

"When Bo was born, he didn't have any hair on top, just on the sides and back," Martina said. "The doctor held Bo up, and Guy said, 'Look, he's got my hair!' Kenny and Guy were two very different people, but both were hysterical."

Smith does not have one regret from the two years he spent in Denver with Kenny.

"Kenny is an inspiration to what you can be, not what you want to be," Smith said. "There is a difference there when you think about it. I'm the luckiest person I know because I was able to work with him as long as I did."

Smith can't shake the feeling that had Walker survived Stautner's tenure, Walker would be a perennial Pro Bowl player at this point.

"I've been a football fan my whole life, so while I didn't know as much as a coach, I know a lot more than the average fan, especially after working with Kenny and the Broncos those two years," Smith said. "And I realize that I might be viewed as biased because I got so close to Kenny, but I can honestly say that he was as quick as any defensive lineman I ever saw. And Kenny was stronger than any person I ever saw. His motivation and drive were unmatched."

When the Broncos beat the Green Bay Packers to win the Super Bowl in January of 1998, no one was cheering harder than former Bronco Kenny Walker. While he was not happy to be released, he is still grateful that Denver gave him a chance to realize his dream of playing in the NFL.

"I was very happy to see Denver win the Super Bowl," Kenny said. "I actually dreamed in September (of 1997) that the Broncos were going to win the Super. But I dreamed they were playing the 49ers. I was happy for those guys, especially the ones I knew like John Elway. It was good to see Pat Bowlen get a Super Bowl. I met so many people in that organization that were just great to me, that I have good feelings for that club. I will always be a Broncos fan."

CHAPTER 13

FATHER AND HUSBAND

While Kenny was getting his pro football career started, he missed Martina and Tommy. Talking on the telephone through the telephone-typewriter phone relay (TTY, which involves an operator telling the hearing person what the deaf person is typing and then typing to the deaf person what the hearing person is saying), Martina got the impression Walker wanted her and Tommy to move out to Denver.

"He was at training camp," Martina said. "To this day we still don't know if it was a misunderstanding. We were talking on the TTY. He had told me—or I thought he indicated to me—that he wanted me to move out there. I really missed him. I thought he was saying he could get married now."

"What I was saying," Kenny said, "was that I missed her and wanted to get married, but not until I was 25—that's when insurance rates go down."

Kenny knew early in his career as a pro football player that he would never choose football over family.

"I remember a coach's wife asked him about coaching football," Kenny said. "She said, 'Do you love football?' He said that he did. She asked, 'What is the most important thing in your life?' And he said, 'You know what it is—football.' I thought to myself, 'How can that be?' It made me re-evaluate my priorities. I wasn't going to split that much time and shortchange my family for my work. Family and football—ask me what is more important, and I will tell you in a split second that family is far more important."

In October of 1991 Kenny and Martina got engaged. On Valentine's Day, February 14, 1992, Martina and Kenny married.

Life as a pro athlete was taking a toll on Kenny. While he was lonely during the late evenings, he was so busy during the day that he felt like he didn't have time to count his toes and fingers.

"It just seemed to me that too much was happening too fast," Kenny said. "There was so much pressure. I had a new house, a new car, and from 8 a.m. to 5 p.m. I was worried about the clock—where I had to be at any time. Then I'd just go home for the night and forget about everything. I was just so busy that my head was spinning. I was worried about having to use the phone because I had to use the relay, so even though it is a great service for deaf people, it is not a completely private thing."

Even though having Martina and Tommy in Denver helped Kenny adjust to his new life, he still wasn't able to put a lot of effort into his relationship.

"In professional football you have it all in terms of money," Kenny said. "But it's hard to have a relationship when you are a professional athlete. It's a hard life for the family."

Since Tommy was just a baby when Kenny and Martina met, they did not have a tangible relationship. However, by the time Martina and Tommy joined Kenny in Denver, Tommy was four years old.

"Kenny would never hurt him, and Tommy likes Kenny," Martina said. "They had a really good relationship when we were just dating in Nebraska. But when Kenny became his father, it was different. It was rough for a while. They didn't get along. Kenny loved him and cared about him. But their personalities were different. Tommy was like, 'You are not going to step in here and tell me what to do. My mom and I can make it alone.' "

There were humorous times. Kenny had developed a customized, efficient form of sign language with Mimi Mann and Guy Smith. Like anyone else, Martina had her own idiosyncrasies when it came to signing—and cooking.

"She thought she was a great cook," Kenny said with a smile, "but when she made rice the first time, it was crunchy. Now, she interprets well, and the rice is much better, too."

"He told me a few years later that he knew I messed up the rice, and he just ate it anyway because he appreciated my effort and didn't want to appear ungracious," Martina said.

While Tommy was adjusting to Kenny, Kenny was also adjusting to being a father figure for the first time. Kenny was the youngest in his family, so he had never been in a similar situation.

"Kenny was wondering why Tommy would do the things he was doing," Martina said. "Tommy does not like sports like Kenny. They struggled for a few years—of course Tommy was only four-and-a-half-years-old when we got married. When we were in Denver, we bought bunk beds for Tommy because it was something he wanted. You have to understand that Tommy is very dependent on routine and stability, and moving to Denver was very hard on him. We had a hard time getting him to bed at night. Kenny thought it might perk Tommy up if he decorated Tommy's bunk beds with Christmas lights. Kenny and I were watching TV and didn't hear anything—it was quiet for 45 minutes. We went and checked on Tommy. He had taken out every light bulb and put them in a pile. Kenny and I just threw our hands up in the air. It was a big adjustment for Tommy. In Kenny he had a full-time father for the first time. Tommy got jealous a lot."

Some people might believe that taking on the role of father was hard on Kenny. But he was mature enough to know that he was fortunate to have Tommy.

"You have to accept people for who they are and those who love them," Kenny said. "I loved Marti, and so I would love her son, too. That was the hardest part for me. I would have liked for things to be easier, not having the child. I became a father right away to a four-year-old son. I didn't know if I had that in me to do, since I was still young. Now, I can imagine it no other way."

Kenny had experienced a lot of things Tommy would go through.

"It is frustrating raising a deaf child," Kenny said. "I have learned about deafness since I was two years old. If you are around the kids, you have to have a lot of communication. You focus on his needs. You have to really concentrate on the learning process and coordinating the whole thing. You have to use a lot of common sense when you are deaf. Sign languages are different. Deaf adults were having difficulty reading and writing. English is the most difficult language to sign."

Kenny said getting used to appreciating Tommy's own interests took some time.

"It took me a lot of patience to work with him," Kenny said. "His personality is to be really shy. The big problem for me, being a father, is I wanted to teach him sports, and he had very little interest in sports. I learned that it just doesn't always happen that way. You expect all these things from kids, but you can't just make it happen and make them a certain way because you want them to be that way, or because you had a certain interest or ability. Part of me felt like a failure as a father because I couldn't get him to play sports, and it's just not that way."

Martina said the trio persevered through some tough times.

"I don't blame Kenny because it was hard on him, too," Martina said. "I was in the middle of it all the time. I went to a counselor."

Since Tommy's father was not around him very often, Kenny was the first adult male in Tommy's life, aside from Martina's father, Dan Offenburger.

"Kenny was fairly strict with Tommy," Offenburger said. "He placed expectations on him. We felt that was good. Tommy didn't always like that. You have to realize how close Tommy and his mom are. Any kid with a single mom is very close to her. Add the deafness and the frustration that brings, and you see why that bond was so strong."

Tommy, Dan said, was a perfect fit for Kenny, even though it didn't seem like that at first.

"A young deaf child is hard to deal with," Offenburger said. "Tommy had an explosive temperament. You had to deal with him firmly. Sometimes it was hard to feel good about disciplining him so harshly. But we knew it was for his own good."

The parenting skills needed for a deaf child aren't unlike a lot of the child-rearing practices for a hearing child.

"One thing we learned with Tommy is that you always give him an option," Offenburger said. "You don't just say, 'Eat your dinner or I will spank you.' You give him an option, 'Eat your dinner and see a movie? Or don't eat dinner and go to bed?' "

Offenburger believes that Tommy will have a greater chance to succeed in life because of Kenny.

"Kenny exerts a great influence on Tommy," Offenburger said. "Tommy can see how self-sufficient and independent Kenny is, and that makes Tommy see that he can have that one day if he can be driven and work hard like Kenny always has. Kenny was a definite positive influence."

Kenny's celebrity as a player for the Denver Broncos was both a plus and a minus in his relationship with Tommy.

"We went to preschool graduation. When we showed up at Tommy's school in downtown Denver, they had a nice picnic outside," Martina said. "Kenny had gotten a lot of media coverage, so when he showed up, a line formed in front of Kenny for autographs. Tommy went over and sat on a swing with his head down, looking at Kenny as if to say, 'You stole my day.' Kenny noticed that, and he politely said, 'I am here for my son Tommy. I will autograph for you all later after graduation. But not now.' "

After working intensely on communicating during the summer of 1997 in a "home school" format, Kenny and Tommy took their relationship to a new level. The work was hard, but rewarding.

"Tommy has improved so much, and Kenny applauds Tommy's effort and the strides he has taken," Martina said. "Kenny's relationship is different with Tommy. He can relate to him in ways that I can't. He can tell what Tommy is feeling—you can see the love."

Having two of his own children with Martina has been nothing but a million smiles a day for Kenny, who seems to live to spend time with the children.

"Kenny loves Bo and Anna so much," Martina said. "Bo interprets for Kenny with the babysitter. But we have to be careful with Bo because we don't want him to feel like he has to have all that responsibility. He does it because he loves his father and wants to help him however he can. Bo and Anna can understand Kenny. Anna tries to sign. He does miss a lot of what she says. Bo used to be like that, but now they communicate a lot better."

While Kenny loves Bo and Anna as much as anything in the world, he is just as proud of Tommy.

"I'm not worried about Tommy because I know he will do fine," Kenny said. "It took a lot of years to get to this point. I had to find a way to teach him because at first he'd use body language. I had to show him so he could learn with his eyes. It took him years to develop it and to accept the discipline and patience. His discipline has really grown and improved as he responded better. He pays attention better. A lot of times he would be daydreaming and not focusing. It took so many years to build up his ability to focus. He finally opened up. But I understood the difficulties because that's how my life was."

CHAPTER 14

RELEASED BY DENVER

Certainly, since Walker had survived until the final cut of the Denver Broncos, another team would pick him up. Certainly, since Walker was a starter in 1992, he would get at least a workout from a dozen other teams. Certainly, one of these scenarios would unfold, right?

Certainly not.

"The day after the Broncos cut me, a team called to see if they could evaluate me—work me out," Kenny said. "I had packed my bags. Then they called my home, telling me not to come because they didn't want to deal with having to hire an interpreter."

The situation turned far bleaker far sooner than Walker could have ever imagined, even in a possible worst-case scenario.

"I was hurt because I was running out of hope," Kenny said. "I was supposed to go to workout for another team, but that didn't work out, either. I didn't have a lot of options left. I kept asking, 'Why me?' If I would have gotten one workout, I could have made a team."

One of the hardest parts of living in Denver—unemployed—was seeing the Broncos each Sunday on TV.

"I watched that season's games on television," Kenny said. "We still lived in Denver, and it was so hard to watch the games. I knew things weren't right, that I could still play in the league. There were a lot of things that didn't add up. We saw defensive ends getting hurt and dropping like flies on a lot of teams. It seemed like more defensive ends were hurt that year than had been in a long time. My agent would call those teams the following week, but no one wanted to even work me out."

Call after call was made on Kenny's behalf. Each time a "No thanks" was extended—at least it was when the calls were returned, which was not always the case.

"Another of my agents said he would go to his grave frustrated from having doors closed in his face," Kenny said.

The abrupt ending was what Kenny was struggling with more than anything else.

"There was just some unfinished business there—it was just gone all of a sudden," Martina said. "He went from being a starter one year, to not even being able to get a workout with any team the following season. His agent would ask, 'Could he even just get in his sweats and run the 40-yard dash? Could you look at some film?' The answer was always no."

When the Broncos top draft pick was lost for the season with a serious knee injury, Kenny figured he would get his chance. Once again, he figured wrong.

"You don't think of a guy being released after being a starter," Martina said. "He kept working out. Then their top draft pick, Dan Williams, a defensive end, blew out his knee. Kenny knew the defense, coaches and the players. So we were pretty sure he'd get a call."

Despite all the doors shutting in his face, Kenny believed he would still play in the NFL that season. Even Martina did not want to move because it seemed logical that Kenny, getting stronger every day through his intense workouts, would return to the Broncos or another team.

"The first season, we still had hope," Martina said. "We were pretty sure someone would pick him up. I knew he was upset, and I wanted him to continue. I learned a lot more about football. Kenny would explain to me what was going to happen. He could really read the defense."

While the family's world had been turned upside down, Martina still believed that in time Kenny's career would get back on track.

"It was really difficult for me, more difficult than I can explain," Martina said. "I felt like it was a mistake to cut him. It seemed like for three weeks I was really bored. I had this routine established, and I really expected it to be that way. I had every reason to believe it would work out."

The whole family had to deal with the storm of uncertainty surrounding the situation.

"It all happened so fast," Martina said. "When you lose your job, it's a trauma to the whole family. There was no place to work off all the steam I had. I would call his agent, and for some reason the teams just weren't calling back—week after week without a response."

When the Walkers moved into their Denver home after Kenny's rookie season, they had no idea that 18 months later they would be headed back to Nebraska. But without many other options, the Walkers did just that, heading to Lincoln in October of 1993.

Kenny went back to finish his schooling at the University of Nebraska.

"The life in Denver was too expensive," Martina said. "So we had to move. I wasn't depressed; I was mad."

As the money wore down along with Kenny's possible shots of hooking up with another team, the Walkers had to start dealing with the reality that their time in Denver was over.

"Soon, there were so many other things to worry about," Martina said. "The first was we had to uproot the family and move."

Moving had been the last thing on Kenny's mind as he prepared for training camp that summer. Yet, when October rolled around, Kenny realized he had to attend to his family.

"At the time, what could I do about it?" Kenny asked rhetorically. "I had to worry about my family, about a preschool for Tommy. So it was about a lot more than football."

There was one more chance to play professional football, but it would not be in the NFL. Officials from the Canadian Football League were surprised to see a player one year removed from starting in the NFL out of the game altogether.

"In 1994 my agent called the Canadian Football League," Kenny said. "I knew almost nothing about the CFL."

The Hamilton Tiger Cats pounced on Walker. His heart was not completely into heading north of the border. At the same time he had yet to really develop a career off the field. So football was still an appealing option, even though Kenny wasn't looking forward to the uncertainty and new surroundings the move to Hamilton brought.

"I wasn't that thrilled, but it was better than nothing," Kenny said. "It was an opportunity to get some film, build up some statistics and then go back to the NFL. I really wanted to play football again, in the NFL. This was going to help reach that goal. "

So Kenny joined the Hamilton Tiger Cats.

"I was happy at times, but it was like I knew I had to have more to do with my family," Kenny said.

That feeling wore on him more and more as time passed.

"We went up to Hamilton before training camp," Kenny said. "I wasn't really comfortable with the whole thing. It was different than NFL football. The players were smaller, and the field was longer and wider. It was too much change for me. There was a lot more running during the game. I had put on weight to get bigger because I needed more size to be a lineman in the NFL. I hadn't done as much running as I used to. Since I didn't play on special teams my second year with the Broncos, I had done less running that season than the first."

Just as the field was different, so was the kind of conditioning needed for the more wide-open game, which relied more on speed and less on big-bodied linemen than the NFL.

"It was difficult to get in the kind of shape I needed to be in for the CFL," Kenny said. "And the fact is you have to be in top condition to play. The CFL is not about strength as much as it is speed because of the wider and longer field."

But as far as football was concerned, Walker was more than holding his own on the field.

"It went well the first three weeks of Hamilton's training camp," Kenny said.

In a preview of things to come, Kenny found out his new home was about to become his old one.

"Calgary traded a couple of offensive linemen for me because Hamilton had a bad offense, and Calgary needed a good defensive lineman," Kenny said.

The move to Calgary was another shock for Kenny as his surroundings again changed. However, the same conditioning problems he experienced in Hamilton followed him, at least initially, to Calgary.

"I was doing pretty well, but I was still not in good shape, and they ran us even more in Calgary than they did in Hamilton," Kenny said. "I was about 280 pounds, and I was exhausted by halftime."

Without a Mimi Mann or Guy Smith, Walker was forced to adjust to his new surroundings and open new lines of communication with new teammates and coaches on his own. Martina and the children, who had just moved to Lincoln with Kenny before he got the call from Calgary, stayed behind until Kenny was sure he wanted to give it a go in the CFL.

"I enjoyed the city of Calgary," Kenny said. "I liked the club and my teammates, but I wasn't that happy. The team didn't pay for an interpreter, so that made things a little difficult. Everything seemed to be going fine, football-wise. But they were asking a lot more than I had grown accustomed to. Because they have so few players on CFL teams compared to NFL teams, you have to play on special teams."

His heart was getting worn out, emotionally as well as physically.

"I was away from my family, and at that point in my life, that was the last thing I wanted," Kenny said.

Things were going very well in Calgary, despite the communication problems and not having an interpreter.

"I could tell Kenny was a bit frustrated already because to not have an interpreter was hard to deal with," Martina said, "especially with the situation in Calgary where the coach didn't try as hard as he could have to help Kenny."

Kenny made it through the first year, starting as the Stampeders made it all the way to the semifinals of the CFL Championship. Despite an impressive season, Kenny was still not getting any interest from NFL teams—not even a nibble.

After the CFL season ended, Walker came home, took a job cutting plastics at a factory from 11 p.m. to 7 a.m. and went to school at the University of Nebraska to finish up his degree.

Martina was pregnant at the time with Anna. Kenny worked off his tuition by making appearances and then supervising study hall at the university in the evening.

"Sleep was a few hours here, a few hours there," Kenny said. "I was getting about three hours of sleep a day."

Martina was proud of her husband's effort to better himself and provide for his family.

"Kenny is, along with my father, the hardest-working person I know," Martina said.

When Kenny reported to Calgary for his second CFL season on August 17, 1995, he knew it was better for his wife, who was seven months pregnant, to stay in Iowa with her parents nearby, and with Bo and Tommy. But Martina could hear the loneliness in Kenny's voice when they spoke on the phone. She wanted to move up there, but Kenny could not take leave from the team during the camp. While 1,600 miles separated them, Martina planned to close that gap with a mini-van and a U-haul trailer.

"We were talking on the phone, and I said, 'Are you crazy or just stubborn?'" Kenny said. "A couple of days later, I open my door, and I see this huge pregnant woman with a van and a U-haul. The van was a mess, the kids were arguing."

"Bo was only two years old at the time," Martina said. "But he saw Kenny, and he started running to him."

"I was happy to see them—especially that they were safe," Kenny said. "I was so worried about her. When she got here, I was relieved."

The Calgary defense was ranked at the top of the CFL in most categories. But Kenny was down emotionally.

"We were such a long way from home," Kenny said. "I would see the NFL games on television and think I was settling for less. I started to change as a person. I was playing in the CFL just to get some statistics to show to NFL teams so I could get a chance to play again. But that was not going to work out, and I had yet to accept that fact."

The Calgary offense more than held its own with long-time CFL star Doug Flutie leading the team to a 13-0 record. With four games left in the season, Kenny was looking forward to getting the championship trophy that he had narrowly missed out on at Nebraska and in Denver with the Broncos.

But in the end of September, things changed.

Martina met with Kenny and his coach and told the coach that Kenny could contribute a lot more to the team's success if the coach could do the little things that helped Kenny—like facing him when he talked to Kenny, or taking some time before or after meetings to go over things with Kenny.

"He didn't seem real interested in what I was saying—I was sure of that just by the mannerisms and his attitude," Martina said. "I said, 'Kenny is working his tail off. He wants to stay here, but we keep hearing rumors that he will be traded.' Even though he had been told he needed to face Kenny, he would always turn his back and talk as he wrote on the chalkboard. By that time, he had made his decision that he was going to trade Kenny, and he was trying to justify what was going to happen, saying what Kenny was doing was wrong. He just blamed everything on Kenny. Kenny said, 'I don't understand him half the time,' and I told the coach. The coach said, 'Oh, yes he does.' Kenny said, 'No, I really don't. But I want to.' The coach said, 'I will take care of this.' "

The coach did on the next day, trading Kenny—who had twice been named the CFL's defensive player of the week while in Calgary—to Winnipeg, long the CFL's doormat, for former Denver Broncos' backup quarterback Shawn Moore. There were only five games left in the regular season.

"The coach called, and I answered the phone," Martina said. "He knew he could get Kenny by going through the relay service. But he didn't want to have to deal with Kenny. I answered the phone and he said, 'We traded Kenny to the Winnipeg Blue Bombers. Good luck.' He hung up, and that was it." Martina had many thoughts racing through her mind, but she held her tongue.

"I didn't say anything," Martina said. "There was nothing to say. I just had to let it go. We thought, 'Winnipeg? They are one of the worst teams in the league.' Anna was six weeks old. I tried to adjust 'OK, me and the kids in Calgary, alone. This is going to be tough.' "

Kenny did make the most of what he did learn in Calgary. Twice he was named Player of the Week, earning a microwave oven and a color TV for three sacks.

A friend on the team, Mark Pierce, was from England and was a blacksmith by trade. He made beds with iron frames, which Kenny liked.

"He didn't have a TV and microwave, and we didn't have a very nice bed, so we traded," Kenny said. "Wood posts and an iron frame—we have it to this day."

Kenny said the fact that the Calgary coach was also the team's general manager made it hard for Walker to get a fair shake pleading his case.

"It's kind of a conflict for a coach to be a general manager," Kenny said. "There are two sides there, and you want to talk to the coach, but he's wearing his general manager hat. So you want to talk to the general manager, and then he talks to you like the coach."

If the Calgary coach was sick of dealing with Kenny, he must have at least known the feeling had unfortunately become mutual.

"With the communication problems, I started to tire more and more of the business end of pro football," Kenny said. "I kept asking myself, 'What do these coaches want?' "

Doug Flutie had a few nagging injuries, and Calgary needed a proven quarterback, which it found in Moore. Winnipeg's defense was among the worst in the league and figured it would get an immediate boost from Walker.

"I had more sacks in the final four games than anyone else on the Winnipeg defense had the entire season," Walker said, "so I felt like things were getting done."

Winnipeg's season ended quietly a month later. But Kenny's play spoke volumes.

"He ended that season like gangbusters," Offenburger said. "At the start of the next season, the Winnipeg coaches thought he was going to be the best defensive lineman in the CFL. Doug Flutie had been traded to Toronto, and Kenny sacked him twice. But his heart wasn't in it."

Calgary, predicted to be a near lock for the Grey Cup, lost in the semifinals to Baltimore, a team that Calgary—with Walker on defense—had pounded not once, but twice during the regular season. In fact, it was against Baltimore that Kenny recorded three sacks in one game and earned CFL Defensive Player of the Week honors.

"I liked the team and the players and coaches," Kenny said. "But in a lot of ways, I just didn't like football anymore. Anna had just been born. And especially after Anna was born, I needed to be with my family."

Kenny came back to Shenandoah and prepared for his life after football. His work ethic from college took him to new heights.

"It was time to really get my career going," Kenny said. "As much as I didn't want to think about it, there were times when I realized football wasn't going to be a part of my life forever."

He worked 20 hours a week making an 80-mile commute to a job at a center for juvenile delinquents in Tarkio, Missouri. He'd do that from 8 a.m. until noon. Kenny would get back to Shenandoah just after 1 p.m., and sleep until 2:30 p.m. He'd get up, go to work as the residence counselor at the Iowa School for the Deaf—a 40-mile roundtrip north to Council Bluffs—and work there until almost midnight. He was working 12-hour days with two hours of driving daily to and from his two jobs on top of that. He'd get home shortly after midnight and be on the road the next morning again to Tarkio.

"I was tired all the time," Kenny said. "I did that for four months and just slept here and there wherever I could."

His father-in-law saw a work ethic that made him proud of Kenny.

"To see a young father work as hard as he did," Offenburger said, "made me very proud. I was so glad to call him my son-in-law."

Walker's contract was up with Winnipeg. While the long work weeks were taking a toll, he was still able to spend weekends with his children, and he liked being back in the midwestern United States.

"Winnipeg wanted to negotiate because I didn't have a contract for the upcoming season," Kenny said. "I just told them, 'I really don't want to play up there.' "

"Their general manager, a man from the South with a big twang in his voice, kept calling and calling—he just really liked Kenny," Martina said. "I told him, 'You know we appreciate you and how you treated him.' Kenny just didn't want to play in the CFL. He tried once more, 'Come on Marti, what will it take to get him here?' "

Kenny thought about it and realized he still had some desire to play football. He still believed, at least in the back of his mind, that this season would be the one that got him back in the NFL.

"I decided at the last minute to give it a try," Kenny said.

"So I went to Winnipeg on my own and came back after playing six games to help Marti and the kids move into our house in Council Bluffs," Kenny said, sitting in the living room of that very house in 1998. "The kids were getting ready for the school year, and Marti was getting ready to take classes at Creighton."

"During the time we were in Winnipeg, we lived in an apartment that had only one bedroom," Martina said. "The air-conditioning was terrible. We were just so tired and burned out from the whole routine of moving, putting stuff in storage, taking it out of storage, being separated at certain times of the year. The uncertainty was too unsettling for us, and it would be for the children, too. So we decided to get the house here in Iowa."

With everyone settled, Kenny went back to Winnipeg—at least he did physically because emotionally his heart and his thoughts were in the new house with the kids in Iowa.

"It was a homesickness like one I had never felt before," Kenny said. "Bo was at the fun age of four where he was doing all kinds of things. Anna was just a baby, and she was my little girl. Tommy was doing well in his new school at the Iowa School for the Deaf and missed the time I was able to spend with him while I was working there."

Kenny called Martina, a call she suspected was coming sooner rather than later.

"My motivation is gone," he told her. "I don't want to be here anymore."

It was obvious to the coaches that Kenny's heart wasn't in football. He had been moved to the practice squad as his lack of desire started to show through in practice. Winnipeg coach Cal Murphy told Kenny he had to decide if his heart was in it because Winnipeg could not afford to carry his $70,000 salary—far above the CFL average—if Kenny was not going to rededicate himself and become the player he was the year before.

"They handled it well," Kenny said. "So by mutual agreement I left Canada, Winnipeg and football, for my wife, kids and our life in Iowa."

"I was happy he was coming home," Martina said. "It wasn't like we couldn't afford it because he didn't make much money in Canada. The tax rate is more than half, and with what it cost him to live up there, we were not making much money at all. So it wasn't even worth it any longer."

After five years of professional football, Martina was more than ready for Kenny—and their young family—to move on.

"I was happy he was out of football because there was so much stress in the CFL," Martina said. "Leaving Canada was a good move for us."

Still, leaving one career for another brought a lot of concerns, some more pressing than others.

"We had health insurance through a Canadian company when he was with the CFL, but the policy didn't apply in the States." Martina said. "So we had no health insurance until we took out a policy at State Farm, but I had a pre-existing condition, diabetes. Our Canadian friends could not believe that we would worry about insurance—they couldn't believe Americans did it that way."

Kenny stayed at his job as residence counselor at the Iowa School for the Deaf but no longer worked at the juvenile center in Tarkio, Missouri.

"I appreciated the experience at Tarkio," Kenny said, "but I had to leave. My body needed some rest.

"Both jobs fit in with what I wanted to do with my post-football career—I wanted to work with kids who were experiencing some sort of challenge," Kenny said. "Tarkio was a rough place. One night we had to go out in the snow and look for a kid who escaped—the kid got away and didn't even have any shoes on. We found him in a ditch near the highway, and he was allright. The Iowa School for the Deaf is also a challenge. But it is one that I can relate to more on a personal level."

The whole package at the Iowa School for the Deaf (ISD) was just a better opportunity for the Walkers because location was also a factor.

"The benefits were better at ISD, and it was better for my family," Kenny said. "It was better for me, too, because I could communicate with the kids. Everybody signed, so I felt more included. My experience of working in the hearing community is over. I started my career in the deaf community. It's what I feel the most comfortable with. And it is especially nice to be able to see Tommy every day at school."

159

Kenny was all right for the rest of that year—glad to be home with his family, away from coaches he never felt he could completely understand.

"I missed football when I first came back, but I did not miss football in Canada," Kenny said. "I don't think I realized it at the time, but I figured out later on that I would have to deal with the fact that I could no longer play. Since I was able to come back and jump right into a good job in my career field, I was able to put the feelings I was having about how my career ended out of my mind—for a while, anyway."

The realization that his football career was irrevocably over didn't hit him until the fall of 1997, when for the first time since 1982, he wasn't getting into pads for fall practice.

"It wasn't an easy decision to leave professional football," Kenny said. "I have pride. I wanted a championship. But the trophy would not have meant much because I was not happy as a man.

"I was ready to start a new life," Kenny said. "In my mind I said forget football. It was time to move on. I was happy to start a new life. I started to work, which was nice, because I had already worked for the Iowa School for the Deaf and liked it, so that made the move easier."

CHAPTER 15

WHEN IT SUDDENLY ALL ENDS

There is documentation galore about how professional athletes struggle to adapt to the "real world" when their career in sports comes to an end. Various statistics point out that the divorce and bankruptcy rates for former athletes is anywhere from three times to 10 times the rate for men the same age who never played pro sports.

Even though Kenny had done more post-career planning through his job at Iowa School for the Deaf and getting his degree, he still felt an emotional crash when he hung up his pads for the final time.

"When your career is over after being a professional athlete, it is a shock," Kenny said. "You enter the real world, and you are at the same point of a 22- or 23-year-old—if you were smart enough to get your degree. If you were one of the ones who left school without a degree, you still have another year or so of work in front of you, postponing the transition even more—making it that much harder. Even if you have a degree, you have so much ground to make up for the years you lost to football."

Although it was clear in Winnipeg that there would be no turning back once Kenny made the decision to leave, he started having mixed feelings the moment he got back in Iowa. While some might call it the "grass is always greener on the other side" theory, Walker said the rush of playing sports is like a drug that can't be washed out of an athlete's system at the drop of a hat.

"There was still hope that I would come back," Kenny said. "There was always that hope—and in the back of my mind, there is still hope on some days, although I know the reality is that I won't play again, and I should accept that. After I played Canadian football, I realized the window of opportunity was closing in terms of extending my career or returning to the NFL. At that point, it was not possible for me to go back again. We tried to look at it as though, 'We're ready for this.' But the truth is, we—like most players and their families—weren't ready for it. I had been working the jobs and planning for the future, so I would guess that I was a little farther ahead of many players at that point where their career ends. But did all that preparation make the transition easy? No—maybe it made it easier, but it did not make it easy."

University of Nebraska assistant coach Ron Brown never played a down in an NFL game, yet he experienced exactly what Walker went through. Brown said the way careers almost always end—through being released, forced into retirement, or as in Brown's own case, injury—make the transition harder to deal with, especially initially.

"I can relate because I was sure a couple of times I had made an NFL team," Brown said. "That transition is usually coupled with feelings of rejection. People who leave athletics don't normally leave in a grandiose retirement situation after long, illustrious careers. Most leave because they are rejected in some way. There's a sense that you failed, even when friends and family assure you that you haven't. It's a difficult thing that every player in any sport at a high level must deal with."

Husker teammate Pat Tyrance, who went on from Nebraska to play for the Rams, said every athlete faces the challenge of transitioning not just in terms of career, but emotionally.

"I played only one year in the NFL, and I still have a hard time letting go," Tyrance said. "Football was very much a part of who I was. In part, but not totally, it defined me as a person. The transition is tough on anyone. Handling that determines how you will succeed in your post-football life. It is not easy for anyone."

Gdowski was drafted the year before Walker was by New Orleans. Gdowski now sees it from a coach's perspective as he is the quarterbacks' coach for New Mexico State.

"Yeah, I definitely can relate to those feelings and thoughts," Gdowski said. "It's something you do your whole life—it is part of your identity, and then all of a sudden you are out of it. You see it even more with guys who do play in the NFL for awhile. At Nebraska, you are in the spotlight so much, and you get so much attention that to step out of that is hard for anybody."

Even Kenny's father-in-law knew what Kenny was going through.

"I went through that when I was canned as the athletic director at Creighton," Dan Offenburger said. "I was selling flavored ice machines outside of Omaha, hustling to see a school guy to sell it to him to put it into his lunch program. I thought, 'How did I end up doing this for a living? Where did I screw up?' Now, I am working for an economic development agency, and it's very rewarding. Once you get your feet on the ground, you look back and see that everyone has tough times. In my job now, I see people lose jobs at major corporations, lose small businesses or get passed over for a promotion that ends their career. It literally happens to almost everyone at some point."

During his 25 years as head coach at Nebraska, Tom Osborne saw a lot of his former players wrestle with the challenge of rejoining society after playing in the NFL. The better ones—the ones who played more than the average NFL career length of three years—actually have a harder time adjusting to corporate America than the players who play only briefly professionally.

"You see that typically with most athletes," Osborne said. "The longer you stay in the game, there is more transition. A player who is fortunate enough to play into his mid-30s has his whole identity wrapped up in being an athlete. So the longer you play, the more difficult the transition is."

There is no doubt that NFL players know they won't play forever. At the same time, careers literally end every week during the NFL season, and most players don't see it coming.

"The ending is usually rather abrupt—like one day you are playing, and the next day you are not," Osborne said. "It's the same feeling with being a coach for a long time and then leaving the game. What you have associated as your whole self-image closes in a short period of time. Athletes in their 30s find out they are competing against either 21- or 22-year-olds for the same job, or the athlete sees someone his own age who already has six to 10 years of experience in that field—yet the athlete has no experience and is basically starting over. People don't realize the applause ends quickly, and the pats on the back stop just as fast."

Walker endured exactly what Osborne described.

"It is hard to believe I played five years of professional football," Kenny said. "It didn't end the way it was supposed to. All the problems through the years, I thought about them and felt like it wasn't fair. There was supposed to be another ending, a different ending—a better ending."

At the time he left Winnipeg, Walker was very pleased with his decision to leave football.

"By the time it ended, I had played for three teams in three years in the CFL," Kenny said. "It wasn't fun any longer to be away from my family. I worried about the money situation, too. It seemed like the money I was making didn't help things at all. I felt like I was wasting my time."

When he arrived in Iowa from Canada, Walker sat in his kitchen and thought about the future.

"You realize you have to start a career for yourself," Kenny said. "And one day you ask yourself, 'What job am I going to do for the next 20 years?' If you wait to start your career until your football career is completely over, it can be devastating. You go from being on television and in the newspapers to working for a 25-year-old. Most guys won't let themselves do that, which limits their options even more. And you go from getting five-figure checks each week to getting three-figure checks every two weeks. If you don't take care of the money you earn in pro football, you will not have a penny when you leave the game, which limits what you can do and where you can do it even more."

Walker wasn't just searching for what his future held for himself and his family, he was searching for answers to who he was as a person. This coming after five years in which on a weekly basis tens of thousands of people applauded him running onto a football field.

"When I am in trouble, I don't feel good about myself," Kenny said. "I was asking myself, 'Football is gone. Who am I? What kind of a man am I?' I look at all the other guys who were leaving pro ball, and I was in such good shape compared to them. I was still working out as hard as I ever did, and I was getting stronger."

CHAPTER 16

"COACH" KENNY WALKER

What does a man who has spent his life in a constant state of learning do for a living now? Easy. He teaches. Not always in a classroom, mind you.

On the staff as residence counselor and assistant football coach, Kenny Walker is working with kids he can really relate to at the Iowa School for the Deaf. Kenny can look at any of the kids at the school, and it is almost like looking in the mirror. While each child has his own experiences, Walker shares the common bond of deafness with the students. They have the same questions he had, and he is delighted to share answers that he came by on his own, often the hard way.

"I can understand what they feel at times," Kenny said. "At the same time, the most important thing for me to do at first is listen to what is on their mind."

Coaching has been a lot of fun for Walker. It keeps him close enough to the game and lets him feel the sense of accomplishment from seeing all the hard work pay off.

"Coaching at the high-school level," Kenny said, "has been a whole new world for me. It is really something else to teach them the things I had learned from the coaches I had. I saw a lot of funny things in these kids. It took me two years to see improvement in the kids. They've improved a lot."

Improved is probably not a strong enough word—the team has gone from lone win seasons to above .500.

"We went from 1-7 two years ago," Walker said with a huge smile, "to 5-4 this year."

The kids on the team certainly took pride in their accomplishments. So does their assistant coach.

"That felt really good for me," Kenny said. "We won the

homecoming game, and we hadn't done that for a while. They will remember that for a long time."

Like Walker's mentor, Tom Osborne, Kenny wants to see continual improvement from the kids he coaches. That doesn't always mean a win on the scoreboard. Rather, it means getting better and making fewer mistakes each week, which—as was the case at Nebraska—means more wins on the scoreboard simply as a by-product of a system centered on continually getting better week in and week out.

"The team really improved," Kenny said. "They learned. They knew that if they gave their best, they would continue to get better. That was really exciting for the other coaches and me. We saw the kids working so hard, and they were improving every week."

One of those not surprised to see Walker enter—and excel at—coaching is current Buffalo Bills head coach Wade Phillips, who coached Walker as the Broncos' defensive coordinator in 1991 and 1992.

"He's the right kind of person to be a coach," Phillips said. "He worked hard. He studied. Usually guys like that become good coaches. He knows how to play the game, and that's the big thing. I knew all along that he would be a great coach if he chose to go into it when his playing career was over."

The superintendent at the Iowa School for the Deaf, Dr. Bill Johnson, said the decision to hire Walker made perfect sense.

"The No. 1 reason we brought him on was that Kenny is deaf, and he was very successful at being a professional football player and a role model," Johnson said. "He is someone who has achieved in an area no other staff person has—pro athletics. We thought this would be good for the kids. After we met Kenny, the attitude he had was just super. So often when you get someone at that level, their ego gets pretty big. Coming down and doing things with kids isn't high on their priority list."

Johnson liked the way Walker always expressed appreciation for the opportunity Johnson gave him.

"Kenny Walker has the attitude of Ken Griffey, Jr., who caters to kids rather than adults," Johnson said. "He was still playing football in Canada, and he said, 'Can I come back after the football season?'

I said, 'That would be fine.' And it worked out great. He came at Thanksgiving and stayed until the end of the year."

After seeing Walker on staff before he left for his abbreviated final season with Winnipeg in 1996, Johnson knew Walker would be a great full-time addition to the ISD staff.

"We jumped at the chance to get him on staff for a couple of reasons," Johnson said. "By then I had seen him work with his kids. He gave everyone attention, working with everyone from gifted athletes to those who were very seriously multiply challenged. He is just super sensitive to the kids. He is an excellent role model. All of those things are great for the program. As it turns out, we could take it one step further—I asked him, 'Would you do some coaching?' Kenny's eyes just lit up. I don't know a better opportunity than having someone like that fall into our lap."

Although Johnson had seen cases where athletes had problems adjusting to the role of coach, he did not foresee that as the case with Walker.

"Sometimes good athletes don't make good coaches," Johnson said. "But his sensitivity to the kids is so good that he shows it on the football field. He takes care of the kids and shares thoughts with them in a positive way. I just see so many positive things he does."

Johnson knew that since Walker had learned about coaching under the very best—Tom Osborne—it would automatically rub off on Kenny, a solid person to begin with. His abilities were nurtured properly by being associated with someone with Osborne's character and perspective.

"I don't have any doubt in my mind that playing for Coach Osborne helped Kenny," Johnson said. "Kenny learned tremendously from that individual. I know for a fact that he has tremendous respect for Coach Osborne, and I believe Kenny carries that over into how he operates. From everything I have read about Coach Osborne, he has a personality similar to Kenny in that he is very caring, sensitive, supporting and encourages everyone around him. That's what Kenny experienced in Lincoln, and he brought that to us."

Walker remembers what Osborne taught him and applies it daily as a coach.

"I remember all the things I learn each day as a coach," Walker said. "Coaching is getting easier every day. I'm not the kind of coach who cusses or yells at the players—I had enough coaches like that after I left Nebraska. I just don't believe in doing that. My job is to motivate them, encourage them and listen to them."

When Kenny called Dr. Johnson as Walker prepared to leave Winnipeg and the Canadian Football League, Johnson took the call as a sign that Walker had found out what is most important in life.

"His priorities were in the right place," Johnson said. "He said, 'I miss my family. I see the younger guys around me have a completely different lifestyle than what I want.' I just think it was great. I can see where his support has been tremendous for Tommy, and Kenny has been a great person. Don't get me wrong, Marti is a good person. But Kenny and Tommy connect on a different level, and that's really good for Tommy—and Kenny."

Johnson knows Walker has struggled at times since leaving the world of professional football. At the same time, Johnson knows all of his staff are struggling with issues in their own lives, meaning Walker is no different in facing life's challenges.

"Kenny has gone through some of the most difficult experiences himself," Johnson said. "He can relate without being preachy. He knows how tough it is not to hear, but still wanting to excel. He knows what it is like to be different. Kenny is willing to plug in there and encourage people because he remembers the positive impact it had when he had people encourage him. He is very willing to help with others. He's just a real pleasure to have on the staff."

Walker is quick to point out that Johnson has given him a good opportunity.

"I am still in a mode where I want to learn, and I know I will always be that way," Walker said. "This job has given me an opportunity to help young deaf people grow, and it has helped me grow as well."

Johnson said Walker is always gracious to anyone who helps him.

"I'm surprised and flattered to think that we've helped him," Johnson said, "because he has helped this program as much as anyone. I know Kenny has been through a lot—I have heard and read the stories. But I see Kenny as a person who is willing to make changes he needs to be successful. I am delighted that he chose us. If this job helps him in his personal life, that's an added benefit."

Former Nebraska coach Tom Osborne said the potential is there for Walker to have a long career in the coaching ranks.

"It sounds like something he likes and enjoys," Osborne said. "He will do a great job, and he can do that a lot longer than he could play professional football."

Walker's wife, Martina, agrees.

"He's found his niche," Martina said. "He's great at his job. He's starting to understand his worth. He knows he can make a difference."

Kenny Walker is also a barber for the kids at school.

"Kenny cuts most of their hair," Martina said. "He does it because he and the kids get such a kick out of it. They just enjoy doing things together."

But don't ask for a haircut unless you have one particular style in mind—the house special.

"It'll be short," Martina said. "His specialty is shaving it."

Kenny makes that difference not just with the top athletes at the Iowa School for the Deaf, but also the ones who aren't on any sports team.

"There is a boy at the school who has a limp and cerebral palsy," Martina said. "Kenny calls him 'Cowboy' because he wears a hat and boots. The boy follows Kenny everywhere. One day I was picking up Tommy after school, and I was looking for Kenny. There he was with this boy, who is very, very handicapped, and Kenny's helping him shoot baskets. The boy's face was just alive and shining with pride. Kenny's the same way with the other kids who have multiple handicaps. He takes them with him to the gym at the school to lift weights."

Mimi Mann, Walker's interpreter in Lincoln, said Walker is in a good situation for now. But she expects Walker to eventually further his education and expand his professional horizons with the deaf segment of society even more.

"I think where he is now is a good job for him because it combines all his strengths—he can do the arts thing and work with children," Mann said. "But there's so much more he wants to do in life, areas he wants to grow in and educational goals he has set. But for now, I think it's something great for him and the kids at the school."

Kenny's father-in-law, Dan Offenburger, said Walker can relate to the kids at the Iowa School for the Deaf because he's been there.

"He's going to face those challenges his entire life," Offenburger said. "Deaf people really get the shaft a lot of times. Those challenges will never be over. He is an extremely sensitive person to those who face handicaps or other physical and emotional challenges."

Mann said deaf people are very analytical in dealing with the situations and challenges they face on a daily basis.

"During every deaf person's whole life, he/she develops coping strategies," Mann said. "They have to deal with serious problems all the time and have to figure out ways around them."

For Walker's mother, Julia, the only important thing is that Kenny somehow remain involved with deaf children. Julia said she knows of no better high-profile role model for the deaf community nationwide than Kenny.

"That's what I wanted him to do from the get-go, to give back what he had gotten from educators and people like Mimi Mann," Julia said. "He knows what deaf children need. He has to work with kids like that and give them all he possibly can to help them achieve, just like so many fine people did for Kenny over the years. There was a woman in Denver, Alice Avstriah. She was just wonderful. She would come to our home and help us with sign language. She was his first teacher. When Kenny finished elementary school and went to junior high, Alice got a job at the junior high. Kenny came back to Texas for high school, but when he was getting ready to leave in August for his first year at Nebraska, Alice went to the Denver airport. Kenny was connecting to Lincoln from Texas through Denver. So Alice went and spent a couple of hours with Kenny during his layover. He's just been so blessed to have those kind of people around him. To this day, we always get a call or card from Alice at some point during the year. When he played for the Broncos, Alice got excited about that and went to see him play."

CHAPTER 17

A FAMILY DEALS WITH DEAFNESS

At the Walker's house in the cozy town of Council Bluffs, Iowa, Martina Walker works her hands at the speed of light at times. She is the eyes and ears for not one, but two deaf people, her husband Kenny and her oldest son Tommy.

"It gets tiresome sometimes," Martina said. "I get tired of being involved in every conversation. If we do something involving kids, Kenny will want to strike up a conversation with every one of them. So that keeps me busy whether or not I was planning to strike up a conversation of my own."

Martina met a woman who was in a similar situation and found that the woman had experienced very similar feelings.

"I have always been a positive person," Martina said. "I didn't think about things being hard to deal with—that didn't even cross my mind. Then one day I was talking with a woman who can hear, and she is divorced from her deaf husband. I listened to her talk about the struggles. I realized what she meant, about how whenever your deaf mate talks to a hearing person, you have to be the interpreter. There were times when I was crying or ill, and I didn't feel like doing it. There were times when all I wanted to do was eat a hot meal, but I couldn't because I had to communicate for Kenny or Tommy. Kenny is a wonderful husband and dad, but I thought about what this woman said, and it helped me realize that the feelings I was experiencing weren't selfish or abnormal. Sometimes I have talked about my frustration."

The deafness also limits what the family can see at the theater.

"I go to a lot of movies alone, or we go to see action movies," Martina said. "I want to see *City of Angels*, but it is a movie filled with dialogue. Now *Titanic*, that was a good movie for Kenny. It had some dialogue, but it was a good movie for him to see. At the end he was sitting on the front of his seat. We took our kids, and they loved it, too. Tommy and Bo were asking about it the whole way home."

Titanic was coming to an area theater with closed-captioning, making Kenny and Tommy eager to see it again.

The deafness takes on a life of its own in the most common of situations. Kenny is an accomplished cook, but he has to pay attention to the clock because he can't hear the timer go off. And if the family's dogs are barking outside, someone has to tell Kenny.

"Even though Kenny can read lips, he can't hear the dogs barking unless he is looking right at them," Martina said.

While some of the scenarios are humorous, there are times when Martina says she is ready to pull her hair out.

"He can't tell I am on the phone unless he sees me talking into it," Martina said. "So he'll be in the back room or kitchen and blow his nose like a trumpet. Or we'll be getting ready to go somewhere, and the phone will ring. Kenny will be yelling, 'Let's go!' as loud as he can, not realizing I'm on the phone."

There are also very serious potential problems.

"Early in May (of 1998), there was a lot of bad weather and Kenny was at home with the kids," Martina said. "The tornado warning sirens went off. Our two younger kids can hear, but they aren't old enough to know what the sirens mean. Although Kenny is very perceptive, I called my neighbor who told Kenny that there was a tornado warning. The neighbors are very helpful with stuff like that."

Still, Martina replays in her mind possible scenarios and tries to think out solutions in advance.

"What would a deaf person do in the middle of the night if a tornado hit?" Martina asked. "Sometimes I have to get ahold of Kenny on a moment's notice, and I can't do it."

The communication gap must constantly be bridged.

"Many deaf students struggle with reading skills, although it has improved a lot," Martina said. "You work on your reading skills and find out what one sentence means. You have to understand it. I really struggled to communicate 'ing' endings and idioms. For example, I would tell Tommy to 'Go wash your hands off.' And he thought he had to literally scrub until his hands came off at the wrist."

Kenny wants to help other deaf people through various ventures, including a bold one designed to link all members of the deaf community.

"Kenny has a lot of ambitious goals to help deaf people," Martina said. "He wants to set up stuff for the deaf community in Council Bluffs, maybe an apartment complex to start with. Having a deaf 'neighborhood' like that would really make some people's lives better. But there are a lot of issues that would have to be dealt with, like if someone is not deaf, it would be against the law to keep them from moving in. So we'll see what we can do."

The deaf community has a lot going for it, some of which the hearing public doesn't fully grasp.

"What hearing people don't realize is that deaf people are so organized," Martina said. "Most people think deaf people are lazy and want things given to them. People with disabilities are the most organized people—they need to be organized, or they can't make it in life. They know what their resources are, but they want to be on their own. They don't want sympathies or handouts, just a chance to succeed."

Kenny offers these tips to people who have deaf friends:

• Find out if your friend is deaf, or hard of hearing. "Some people, like me, who are deaf wear hearing aids, but it just amplifies noise, not words or sounds. People ask me if I am deaf or hard of hearing. In the research they did on me, I am deaf. Even with hearing aids cranked up all the way, all I can hear is noise, like pitches or tones. I can hear no words. Understanding the person's hearing impairment could really help the way you communicate with them."

• If you know the deaf person you are talking to can read lips, talk normally. "Sometimes, people will really exaggerate the way they talk because they think if they talk slower or really pronounce the words with dramatic mouth movement, it will make it easier to read their lips. Just the opposite is true. We learn to read lips in normal conversation. Talk that way. Varying the way you really talk only makes it harder to read lips."

• Face the lip-reading person when you talk to them. "This is something that deaf people face every day. It was hard when the teacher would turn around and face the chalkboard. Just as it is when I am talking to a friend, and they turn to pick something up or look at something else. Once I miss part of the conversation, it's hard to pick it up again right away. Whatever is said after they turn around doesn't always have a context."

• Don't talk louder. "This is actually kind of funny, but some people think if they talk really loud, I will understand them more or better. I am deaf, and I can't hear a word. Even if they had a microphone and speakers it wouldn't help me a bit."

• With deaf children—or adults—be aware that there might be other challenges. "Sometimes deaf people have additional handicaps, whether it is autism or another learning disability. At the same time, don't assume they do have another disability—because someone is deaf does not mean they are mute, and it certainly does not mean they are dumb, either."

• Remember the sense of isolation deaf people feel when they are in a group of hearing people. "It is like what happens at the dining room table where the deaf person misses part of the story and never catches up. Don't say to the person, 'Oh, never mind' because it really makes them feel excluded, which they already do feel to a degree because they are deaf. I have felt isolated so many times, and that is one of the hardest things to cope with as a deaf person."

• Feel free to repeat information to give it context. "I can't remember how many times people have said, 'Oh, I told you that before, remember?' Well, I might have missed it for whatever reason. Go ahead and provide as much information as you can in a conversation with a deaf person. Because in a deaf person's life, so much information is wasted because we just don't take it in as readily as the hearing population."

• Don't feel sorry for the deaf, or anyone with a disability. "Deaf people don't want sympathy—it is the last thing we would ever ask for, and something we never would accept. What we look for is understanding, which is by no means sympathy. We want to be able to connect with everyone on the same level. We have developed other areas within our facilities—for example, acute visual skills— that help us make up the difference we lose by being deaf. But just treat us like one of you; that's all we want."

CHAPTER 18

DON'T WORRY, BE HAPPY

Since that December day in 1997 on that gravel road in Iowa, Kenny Walker has been more focused than ever on what matters to him most in life: his family.

"He's very big on respect and family," Martina said. "One of the things Kenny has taught me is that I am not inferior, or superior, to anyone else."

Kenny makes dinner several nights a week and is most comfortable working in the yard, watching his children play.

"He really grew up underneath his mother," Martina said. "I could tell he would be a good father. He learned a lot from her about sewing and braiding hair. That's who was there for him in his life."

Julia Walker said she knew Kenny would be a good husband one day, especially when it came to helping around the house.

"It was very important to me that all four of my boys be that way," Julia said. "They all cook and clean and can take care of themselves. They were taught to be neat."

His mother also knew Kenny would be a good father.

"He's a very loving, kind and considerate person," Julia said. "He's very lovable. Look in his eyes, and you will fall in love with him. Something about his eyes and his heart are very special. I still worry some because I am his mother, and I just want him to be happy. I just hope whatever he decides is a good choice."

Kenny's father-in-law, Dan Offenburger, said everyone faces challenges, and neither Kenny nor Martina is any different.

"Kenny is a high-quality person who has gone through a lot of things that are frustrating," Offenburger said. "Kenny Walker is very beloved in our family. We're an open-emotion family."

Kenny has also spent a lot of time reading the Bible in the past year.

"There is a picture of Jesus at my grandmother's house," Kenny said. "I saw Him for a long time, and didn't know who the guy was. But I always thought to myself, 'I'd like to get to know Him more.'"

Now, he gets sustenance and strength from reading the Bible.

"I started taking time to sit and read the Bible and write down parts of the scripture and try and interpret what it means to me," Kenny said. "I learned a little more about Christ in college. Since college I have been keeping the journal. It has helped me as a father and a person. I needed to learn more about God and how to do the right thing in starting a Christian walk. I still try."

He is more spiritual than religious. He believes his deafness stunted his spiritual growth when he was younger. His roommate at Nebraska, Jon Crippen, got Kenny interested in attending church.

"Jon Crippen asked me if I went to church," Kenny said. "I said, 'There's no use in me going.' He told me they had an interpreter. So I was eager to go. I felt like I fit right in. I felt good about it. I really did. I had a long ways to go in working to become a good Christian. When I was growing up, my family always went to church. I didn't really know what was going on. I didn't know what they were talking about. The whole time I grew up, there were no interpreters in my family's church. So I found church to be boring because I did not know what was going on.

"It makes me feel so good," Kenny said. "I felt a strong sense of spirituality, which I was not able to feel before."

Playing under Coach Tom Osborne at Nebraska also nurtured Kenny's faith.

"Coach Osborne is a very good man, a good, honest man, one of the best coaches ever in football—in my mind, he is far and away the best coach ever," Kenny said. "He was a good, Christian man."

Walker's mother believes Kenny revisited his Christian faith at just the right time.

"God has a way of settling you down," Julia said. "Maybe that is what happened. He got in touch with the Lord."

Those who know him the best say Kenny has always tried to lead a Christian life. His football coach at Crane High School, Rickey White, still holds Kenny close to his heart.

"I think about him quite a bit because I really do think about all my players," White said. "There are special ones who you hold a little closer to your heart, and Kenny is one of them. I loved him like my own son."

Walker's actions often spoke louder than others' words.

"One time I was moving from one house to another. He came over and helped me move," White said. "He'd come over and eat with us. He was like one of my own. He always liked helping people, and that stands out about him as much as anything else."

While Walker claims to have learned a lot from his coaches, his coaches also learned a lot from him.

"What is the biggest thing I learned from Kenny Walker?" Coach White said. "Compassion. He has compassion for everyone he meets. It is a big part of who he is as a person."

White also sees Walker as a sort of poster boy for the U.S. Army saying, "Be all that you can be."

"Kenny did not set out to do this, but he proved a point," White said. "People think they can't do something and want to take the easy way out—I would point out Kenny to any of those people. Whether you are handicapped or whatever, you can do whatever you put your mind to."

His coach with the Broncos still reflects on the time he spent with Walker.

"He had a big heart—he was just one of those guys who doesn't come along all that often who had a big heart," said Wade Phillips, now the head coach of the Buffalo Bills. "That's what made him special because a lot of players have talent. But the ones who have heart—whether they can hear or not—are the ones who leave the biggest impression. Kenny was one of those players. It was super for us. You can't expect to experience those kinds of things in life. So it was an experience that all of us won't soon forget."

Kenny Walker has learned a lot about himself and other people through his successes and failures.

"To communicate completely normally with the mainstream public, you have to have the gift of speech and hearing," Kenny said. "It's like if you are going to go into music, you need to get the right sense of rhythm. For communicating, I didn't get the God-given gift I needed, but I tried to make up for it by working as hard as I could and always being accessible."

Walker says he used the same principles for all of his successes, from Academic All-Conference in the classroom at Nebraska to first-team All-American on the field and into the NFL and CFL as a professional player. Walker says these traits are the most important:

• Patience: "I have had to ask people to be patient of me, so I always try to be patient for other people. It is said that patience is a virtue. Through having people in my life like my coaches—Rickey White at Crane, Tom Osborne and Charlie McBride at Nebraska— I have really been able to see the true value that comes with patience. Usually, being patient just means being human. Not everyone can keep your pace, whether it is in a conversation, in the classroom or on the football field. At the same time, you can't keep pace with them at all times. If you both have patience, your relationship—and your own personal growth—will continue to improve."

• Hard work and persistence: "Nothing in life is easy. I had to study more than a lot of students, and everyone knows that I had to get a lot of extra instruction in football. You can translate that to your own life. If you work hard and persist, you will earn what you deserve. There are no shortcuts in life, so there is no point in even looking for them. If you look for shortcuts, you are cheating yourself out of the full experience and reward, not to mention the sense of accomplishment."

• Honesty: "I can deal with the bad news any day. I can't deal with lies. And I would never lie to anyone about anything. Even if the truth hurts, you can deal with it and move on if you know the truth. With a lie, you end up lying again and again. You lose your credibility and your sense of what is right and wrong. Lying is a shortcut that leads to a dead end in all cases."

• Communication: "My whole life is about communication. Most problems can be thrown out the window if you can successfully communicate. You have to be able to communicate to succeed in life. Sometimes it means expressing yourself. Other times it means listening. Never be afraid to communicate."

• Have diverse interests and fully develop your skills: "One of the reasons I was able to always feel good about something is because I always had plenty of interests. I liked school and sports, and I put my family above everything. When football went badly, I still had my family and my art. When I struggled in school, I took more satisfaction from achievements in football. Develop what you do well because it can compensate for your weaknesses—and you should work on your weaknesses, too, of course. I am good with my hands, and I have excellent visual skills—and that's good because I'm not real good with my ears as you know!"

• Always look for opportunities to learn: "This is the greatest thing in life, to me. Learning is such power and gives you such a good sense of self-esteem. Life is about learning, and it helps you keep a keen and open mind. Continuous learning helps you grow as a person."

• Ethics and principles: "This is like the honesty factor in a lot of ways. But it also means treating other people the way you want them to treat you in return. There are some things that are just wrong to do—so don't do them. Don't get involved with drugs because it is wrong and against the law. Do listen to your parents and teachers because it is the right thing to do, and you will learn about life that way."

• Stay in shape: "I viewed lifting weights and working out as more than just a hobby. It makes you feel healthy, and I believe it is one of the reasons I was able to have no surgeries despite playing 10 years of football in college and the pros."

• Don't be impulsive: "I carefully watch how other people react to situations. Think things through before you act. If you react out of emotion, you will probably have consequences that last far longer than the moment of emotion that led you to snap or lose your temper. Remember, you will have to deal with tomorrow what you did today. I am really into analyzing and figuring out solutions. If something happens that I don't like, I want to know why it happened, so I can prevent it or prepare to deal with it in the best way possible in the future. Don't worry—be happy."

LETTERS FROM KENNY WALKER'S FANS

Kenny Walker received thousands of letters during his football career, both at Nebraska and when he played professionally, first in the National Football League and then in the Canadian Football League. Here are a few of those letters:

Dear Mr. Walker,

We are writing in hopes that you will be kind enough to sign a card for us. My son and I write for autographs as a hobby as a way to spend a little time together doing something we enjoy.

Will, my son, blew out a knee in high school, and they couldn't fix it so he could run again. He sort of got down on himself, but after we started this hobby a lot of players had problems and overcame them, and they really picked him up.

He knows about your great ability and talent despite being deaf. You set an example for all people to follow, not just football players. Watching you play makes us all feel good about ourselves.

Please accept our wishes for a healthy and successful career.

Very Respectfully,

Jim and Will

Dear Kenny,

My name is George. I go to Lake Drive School. I am deaf, too. Does your team win?

George

Dear Kenny Walker,

Thank you for signing my card and meeting me. I drew you a picture. I hope you like it. I watch every game you play. You're my favorite player in the whole NFL. Good luck in the game.

Your favorite fan

David

Dear Kenny Walker,

Hi, my name is Jeremy. I am hard of hearing. Kenny you make me feel proud because you are the first deaf player to enter pro football. You play very well! A lot of people in Colorado really like to see you play. I go to a deaf school called Phoenix Day School for the Deaf. Anyway, Kenny, can you please sign this card and send it back? I only have two cards; I wish I had 100 cards of you. You're lucky because I only have two, so it saves you time.

P.S. Can you use a black marker? Thanks!

Dear Kenny Walker,

My name is Kenny. I heard you played football in college and you were deaf. I hope you can be on an NFL team if you make it. I am curious do you have a hard time with football players? I hope that you can develop more skill on defense. You never know, you might make the Hall of Fame! How long would you like to stay in Denver? I will appreciate seeing you on TV saying "NO" to drugs or "Stay in School."

Your friend,

Kenny

Dear Kenny,

I'm writing this short note to tell you of my son Sean. He is 10 years old and weighs almost 100 pounds. He had spinal meningitis when he was two years old and lost 80 percent of his hearing in both ears. He now wears two hearing aids and is doing well in fourth grade. He has some trouble with balance. Two years ago he started playing flag football with no experience but a very good former high school coach. Sean has developed into a very good defensive player. We were following your career at Nebraska and wrote you a letter, but I guess you never got it. My wife went to school with former Bronco Rubin Carter, so we have always tried to follow Denver. You are truly an inspiration to Sean, and we wish you the best of everything.

Yours truly,

Ken

Dear Mr. Kenny Walker,

My name is Miss Gina, and I am a teacher at the Lake Drive School for Hearing Impaired Children. Our school is located in Mountain Lakes, New Jersey. At the beginning of the school year, I began a classroom theme on sports. This unit included learning about all different sports, the importance of teamwork and sportsmanship, and writing to many different athletes. As an athlete, I understand both the importance and reward obtained from athletic participation. My goal is to teach this to the children and that they too can reach any goal despite their hearing loss.

Several months ago I saw a special on one of our networks about you. The children were so excited to learn of a hearing impaired athlete in the NFL!! You are a great role model for all hearing impaired children. The children were so eager to write to you, their hands could not keep up with their thoughts!

Would you please consider writing back to the children and explain what it is like being an athlete in the NFL. They would love to know about your interpreter, where you went to school, when you learned sign language, etc. If it is not too much trouble, maybe you could send an autographed picture to each of the children. Anything you could send or share would be so greatly appreciated!!!

I would personally like to invite you to Lake Drive School anytime you are in the area. We would love to meet a famous athlete! Thank you so much for taking the time to read our letters, and we would love to hear from you. We wish you the best of luck with your football career...Much Success!!!!!

Sincerely,

Gina
Teacher of the Deaf

Dear Mr. Walker,

You are an inspiration. I admire your courage in confronting challenges while living with and overcoming physical difficulties. As a child I lost 90 percent of my hearing in one ear, but this enables me to only partially appreciate the experiences you encounter.

My husband is a big Denver Broncos fan, and he told me about you. Later in the season friends took us to the November Bronco/Seahawk game (my husband advised me against including the score), and I was able to observe you from the sidelines. Then I saw an NFL halftime special on NBC featuring you, which I found very moving.

I hope you will continue to allow reporters and others to invade your personal life so that your story may be told again and again, for you are an excellent role model. Sadly, in this day and age it seems that children often have so little to set their sights upon.

Now that the Seattle Seahawks have eliminated themselves from all likelihood of playoff possibilities, I will be rooting for the Denver Broncos and Kenny Walker. Good luck, and may Santa bring you a Super Bowl ring.

Merry Christmas,

Louise

Dear Mr. Walker,

Thank you very much for visiting my fifth grade class on March 6, 1992. The students were so impressed by you. They particularly enjoyed your sense of humor.

It was wonderful how you patiently waited for each child to use sign language to communicate his name and question. Elizabeth, our deaf child, was the envy of the class after the interview you gave her.

The values you expressed including the importance of family, school and community service had an impact on the class. You are an excellent role model for young people.

Thank you again for an upbeat, entertaining visit.

Sincerely,

Judy

Dear Mr. Walker,

Your visit left a big impression on Elizabeth and all of us. As she gets older and faces difficult times, she can remember your example of success in your profession and your personal life. I think you have a fan for life, and I bet she pays more attention to football from now on, too!

It was great talking to your wife, also. If she (or you) ever has any questions about calling, you can contact me through the school.

Best of luck to you and your family. Have fun with that new baby!

Dear Mr. Walker,

Hello. We are students at the Katzenbach School for the Deaf. We are 9-years-old. Jonathan is 8. We read about you in the newspaper. You are a very, very good deaf football player. You were drafted by the Denver Broncos. Maybe you can teach the team sign language. We hope we see you on TV. Is Denver in the AFC? Maybe you will go to the Super Bowl. We are happy, excited and proud of you.

 Sincerely,

Clement, Andoni, Steve, Tommy ,Jonathan, Jose

Dear Kenny,

You are our class hero. My students wanted to write to you today. The reason that I had been discussing you with my first graders is because of your perseverance.

I gave repeated messages to my students that if they try hard and believe in themselves, they will succeed! You are proof of that!

I showed the students your pictures in People magazine. I sure hope that you continue to influence children positively. They need heroes like you desperately.

I teach with a lady—Pam—who taught you in school when you were 9 years old. She taught with a lady named Alice Avstriah. She said you used to cry because you did not like school!

If by any chance you have a spare minute, could you please write my students a note? Writing is so hard for them. To have their letters answered would be very meaningful to them.

Thanks for all you do, Number 96! Best Wishes.

Paula

Dear Kenny,

I'm not much of a letter writer as you will soon see, but ever since seeing you briefly after the Nebraska vs. CU game, I've remembered some things I've always wanted to tell you. Even if you would have never played in Denver and pursued other things with your life, a lot of other people and I, would have never forgotten you. If I remember correctly, I was a senior, and you had just arrived at Nebraska as a freshman. As you know now, as a senior, you don't have much contact with freshman. But I will always remember the few times I had contact with you on and off the field. You were extremely strong and confident on the field, but very polite off. Many people talk about Kenny Walker's disability, but all I can think of is how incredibly God has blessed you. You will reach, and are reaching, more people than myself or anyone else could ever reach. I have heard so many people talking about you, and I've never heard a negative comment. I hope you can always keep the perspective on life that you have and that you will always be yourself. Never let people change you or take advantage of you because you are polite. Even though you are an incredible example to people, you can wear yourself too thin. And I hear you may have a family on the horizon. If this is true, I hope the very best to you both. I have been married 8 years now and thank the Lord for my best friend, my wife.

Well, I'm living in Colorado Springs now, and I am in Denver at least once a month for business. I just wanted to let you know that there is a fellow Husker nearby, and if you would ever like to get together for lunch or something, I'd be more than happy to join you. If I don't see you, I'm glad I had this opportunity to encourage you and congratulate you on your tremendous success! Take care and God Bless You!!!

Ken Kaelin

EPILOGUE

Dear Kenny,

I have been a football fan from as early as I can remember of my 34 years, but this is the very first time that I have ever written or contacted a pro player personally. I guess it takes a special situation that finally gets me to do something like this.

As you can see, I have enclosed several of your football cards. I would greatly appreciate it if you could autograph one of the cards and return it to the address below. Please keep the other two cards and distribute them as you wish.

You will also find enclosed a picture of my children, Katie and Ben. Please allow me to tell you a little about Katie. Katie was two years old this past July. It is almost exactly a year and a half ago that we found out that Katie has a profound hearing loss. Having never met a deaf person in our lives, this news was quite distressing to my wife, Sharon, and I. Even though we were uncertain what lay ahead, we were determined that we needed good communication with our daughter and she with us. We immediately fitted her with hearing aids, and we all began to learn sign language. We don't know what caused her deafness and assume that she was born with it, but how she became deaf is not important to us. The important thing was to communicate with our daughter, and the quickest and best way to do that was through sign language. We feel very fortunate that we were able to start all of this before she was even 10 months old. As a result, she is signing and reading sign that is appropriate for her age level. Hopefully, her mother and I will keep ahead of Katie for awhile yet as we continue to learn sign with her, but she is so intelligent; I think she's at least going to pass me by in the very near future!

Kenny, I just want you to know that Sharon and I admire you a great deal. Your story is important to make the general public aware of the deaf community and that you really aren't different from anybody else. But more importantly to Sharon and myself and many other parents of deaf children, your story is the encouragement that we need to continue to provide for our deaf child. That whenever we get sad or frustrated or confused or discouraged or even angry about the situation, we must keep in the front of our minds Katie's well-being, and to provide her with as many opportunities as possible.

Thank you so much for your time and consideration. Please feel free to keep Katie and Ben's picture. Peace and joy to you this holiday season and God bless.

Sincerely,

David
Newton, KS